Manage Your Own Career: Make It a SNAPP™

Dr. Donald J. Hanratty

Ron Biagi

Tresa Eyres

It's the How Publishing Company
Dallas, Texas

It's the How Publishing Company

6211 W. Northwest Highway, Suite 2306

Dallas, TX 75225

Printed in the United States of America

10 9 8 7 6 5 4 3 2

Library of Congress Catalog Cataloging-in-Data 2002101816

ISBN 0-9677773-2-1

Contents

Disclaimer

This book is designed to provide accurate and authoritative information with regard to career management.

The purpose of this book is not to cover the whole subject of career management, but to present one approach based on professional experience. We urge you to learn as much as you can by reading, observing role models and consulting with career management professionals.

Every effort has been made to make this book as accurate as possible. Use the techniques and tools as a general guide and not as the ultimate or exclusive source of information. The authors and principals of It's the How, L.L.C. and The Career Control Group, Inc. may not be held liable or responsible to any person or entity with respect to loss or damage caused, or alleged to be caused, directly or indirectly by the information contained in this book. The names and characteristics of all the people used as examples have been altered to protect their privacy.

This book is sold with the understanding that the publisher is not engaged in rendering any type of legal, accounting or financial service. If legal, financial and other expert advice and assistance are required, the services of competent professionals should be sought.

If you do not wish to be bound by the above, you may return this book to the publisher for a full refund.

Internet Feature

You can have online access to the tools and templates in this book. Go to www.careercontrol.com/onlineresources/

About the authors

Dr. Donald J. Hanratty is an entrepreneur, management consultant, volunteer and community leader who has spent the majority of his professional life helping people continue their careers.

In 1984, Don founded The Career Control Group, Inc., a Texas-based firm that coaches hundreds of changing organizations and thousands of individuals each year. Don and his team work with candidates individually, helping them design and develop customized career plans and campaigns that differentiate them and ultimately lead them to satisfying and rewarding work in employment, consulting, entrepreneurial, leisure and volunteer avocations. Don is co-author of *Career Continuation: Make it a SNAPP™*.

Don is also a leader and active participant in career management associations. He is currently on the executive committee of Career Partners International and formerly on the board of directors of OI Partners, the world's largest career transition firm networks. Don was a founding board member of the International Association of Outplacement Professionals (IAOP). Founded in 1988, the IAOP has grown to become the 2000-member International Association of Career Management Professionals.

Ron Biagi is a performance improvement consultant who has spent his professional life helping individuals and corporations succeed.

During his 30 plus years of business experience, Ron has led successful start-ups and has taken established businesses to new heights of profitability and success.

Ron counsels national and international companies, coaching them in the *how* of meeting and achieving their goals. He currently serves on the advisory boards of two U.S. companies. An author, speaker and executive coach, Ron is known for his leadership, discipline and ability to motivate people.

Ron Biagi and Tresa Eyres are co-founders of ITH (It's the How, L.L.C.), a management consulting firm that provides the tools and processes businesses and individuals need to meet and exceed their goals. They deliver interactive workshops and speeches that provide the *how-tos* of meeting and exceeding goals. They are co-authors of *Make It Happen! SNAPP™ Your Way to Success in Business and in Life* and *Career Continuation: Make it a SNAPP™*.

Tresa Eyres is a performance improvement consultant with more than 20 years of experience helping individuals and businesses improve productivity and profitability. She develops programs that increase knowledge, skills and abilities, and she coaches teams in the implementation.

Tresa shares her expertise with individuals and corporations in the U.S. and overseas, helping to foster a well-trained and motivated work force. Programs with Tresa's signature translate the *hows* into simple steps and tools that people can learn and apply.

Manage Your Own Career: Make It a SNAPP™

The principals of The Career Control Group, Inc. and ITH have collaborated to create this book, a tool that merges time-tested career management techniques with the structured project management approach known as SNAPP™. The combination enables individuals to play the career management game from a position of strength.

Acknowledgments

We want to thank the following people for their valuable input during the design, development and review stages. We sincerely appreciate the contribution of each one.

Content contributors and reviewers (in alphabetic order): Denise Caruzzi, Charlie Franklin, Kelly Hanratty, Mary Holdcroft, Tom Kiernan, Steve Leven, Bob Maher, Mark Mitford, Marlynn Murphy, Kathy Pfeiffer, Mary Jo Robinson and John Sell.

Professional services contributors: Jennifer Keith, cover design; Clarence Weems, framework advisor; Jill Eyres, copy editor; Ken Lockerbie, book layout; and the team at Bertelsmann Industries, Inc., printers.

This is our second book together in the series. In addition to the support provided by our content and professional services contributors, we offer a special "thank you" to Chris Harsdorff who has done a wonderful job of keeping us focused and on target.

Preface

A gnome sat on the porch of his little cabin, deep in the far north woods. One rainy day a traveler approached. He noticed the gnome, the cabin and a gaping hole in the roof. After greeting the gnome, the traveler asked, "Why don't you fix that hole in your roof?" The gnome seemed surprised at the question. "When it's raining, I can't fix it," he replied. "When it's not raining, I don't have to."

Career management too often gets the same treatment. When out of work, most people focus on getting a job, but not necessarily on taking the best possible next step toward a strategic career goal (they **can't** "fix it"). When employed, most people focus on meeting the immediate requirements of the job rather than on building that position into something closer to their ideal (they **don't have to** "fix it").

Yet just as a sunny day is the best time to fix the roof, the best time to advance toward your next right career step is now, while you are employed. *Career management* is a life-long integrated process for both succeeding at your current job and realizing your long-range career goals. Effective career management means ongoing planning – always looking two to three steps ahead, even when you "**don't have to**." The process includes periodic career review, personal marketing, score keeping, networking and continuing education. The typical steps in career management can be illustrated with the following diagram.

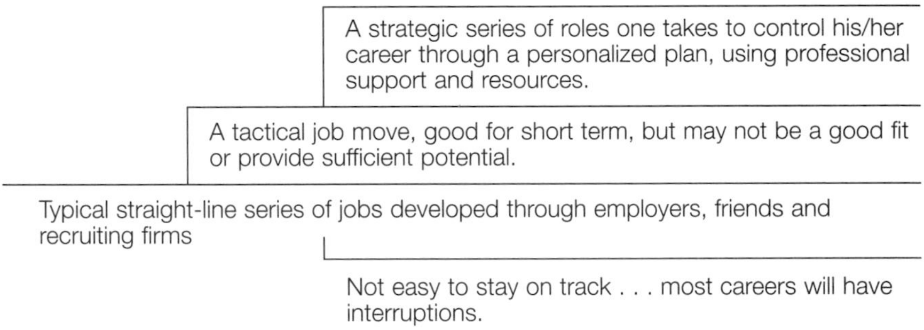

A strategic series of roles one takes to control his/her career through a personalized plan, using professional support and resources.

A tactical job move, good for short term, but may not be a good fit or provide sufficient potential.

Typical straight-line series of jobs developed through employers, friends and recruiting firms

Not easy to stay on track . . . most careers will have interruptions.

Although many think of a career as a straight-line series of jobs developed through a series of employers, friends and recruiting firms (center line), it is not easy to stay on track. Most careers occasionally fall below the main line and experience interruptions. Some diversions above the straight line (first step above) are good for the short term, but may provide only limited potential. The optimal career path (top line) is a strategic series of roles based on a personalized plan that provides opportunities and moves you in a satisfying direction.

Perhaps the most important reason to actively manage your own career is that you want **choices** that lead to greater **control** and **satisfaction**. Most of us are happiest when we have some control over what we do and don't do. When we're happy about what we're doing, we generally are more productive as well. This leads to positive recognition and the opportunity to make the kind of difference we want to see in the world.

The *how* of a well developed and well executed career path is the subject of this book. The Career Control Group, Inc. has developed the framework and practice of career management. In this book, we combine those principles and practices with the discipline of a non-technical, easy-to-follow project management approach called SNAPP™.

SNAPP™ is the five-step process that demystifies project management and helps you develop viable options. SNAPP™ can be applied to any goal you want to achieve. With respect to careers, it combines goal setting, planning and implementation with career management skills such as ongoing self-assessment, strategic planning and resource management.

Success in career management means self-awareness, choices and 100% confidence in your ability and your current step. It arises not only from fixing the roof while the sun is shining, but by making the patch part of the architectural design.

Success rarely happens by itself. The most important ingredient in your success is the degree of responsibility you accept for your own career progress. Once you take full ownership, the guidelines, tips and techniques presented in this book should help you make the right things happen. That is our goal.

—Dr. Donald J. Hanratty
President, The Career Control Group, Inc.
Dallas, Texas

To learn more about The Career Control Group, Inc. and career continuation, visit www.careercontrol.com.

To learn more about It's the How (ITH) and SNAPP™, visit www.itsthehow.com.

Key career management terms and concepts

Job: The description of the specific work you do, usually for an employer. ("My job is developing Web sites.")

Learning organization: An organizational model that directs all employees to act independently and learn how best to do their jobs on behalf of the organization. Dependence on organization charts is replaced by an emphasis on the *values* that support a successfully evolving institution.

Career: Your progress through life with respect to your work. It is the role by which you add value to any enterprise.

Ideal career goal: What you envision now as the pinnacle of your career, the point at which you have achieved everything in your career game plan and are making the difference you want to make.

Strategic career goal: A three- to five-year vision of what you want your work life to be and a step in the direction of your ideal career.

Career management: A life-long integrated process for both succeeding at your current job and realizing your strategic career goals. The process includes periodic assessment, career review, personal planning, marketing, networking and continuing education.

Career development plan: A well-thought out series of scheduled steps to explore and build career-enhancing skills and experiences.

SNAPP™ **:** The simple, non-technical project management approach that helps you get things done within your timeframe and budget. With SNAPP™, you *See* your career as a project with a clear goal, *Negotiate* with yourself and others, *Act on It* by developing a workable plan, *Persist* through successful implementation, and *Praise the Team* (yourself and your network and colleagues) throughout the process.

Success in career management means demonstrating progress toward your strategic career goal while examining and exploring possible next steps. It means self-awareness, options and 100% confidence in your ability and about "where you are" in your career.

Introduction

How do I like my job? Humph. That's why they call it "work."

Only 10 more years, and I can retire.

My job is okay, but I think there's got to be something more.

Thank God it's almost Friday!

Does this sound like you or anyone you know?

If you're like most people, you'll spend 40 to 50 years of your life at work. Doesn't it make sense to enjoy what you do, to find it rewarding and meaningful?

If you're like most people, the answer is yes. You want to be recognized for the good work that you do, and at the end of the day or week or career, you want to think you've made a difference. Doesn't it make sense to manage your career in such a way that you develop choices and have a degree of control about where you ultimately land?

Yet, if you're like many, you feel trapped in your current job and for a variety of reasons can't see a clear way out. Finding a different job may provide a diversion, but unless it is the right job on the right career path, you're likely to find yourself in a similar trap in a short amount of time and no closer to work that will inspire your passion. And the cycle begins again. Perhaps it's happened to you already. It doesn't have to be that way.

Adept career managers have a vision and a plan. They are always thinking ahead about career options even while still challenged and excited about their current work. When the job is no longer fun or when it fails to head in the right direction, they are ready to move.

SNAPP™ shot

Even if you live to be 100, life is short.

Employers have a stake in this career progression as well. Employees who are challenged and excited about their work are the greatest positive contributors to the company's bottom line. It is to the benefit of employers to help employees manage their careers in a way that keeps them highly productive.

While the career game offers no guarantees, taking a structured approach to the process will increase the odds of ongoing job satisfaction while you realize your long-term goals. How can you do that effectively? This book has the answers.

What this book is about

This book answers the need for an up-to-date approach to managing your career while you're working. There are at least three important reasons to do it.

- It is your life and your career. It makes little sense to either put career management aside until you can't avoid it or let someone else take control.
- The employment revolution calls for employees to have a new kind of relationship with the company, thus creating a need for new career management techniques.
- It's wise to make the most of your present situation. You have an investment of time and energy in this job, even if it's a new one. Yet while you feel secure and content in your work, you need to be thinking ahead and preparing your personal marketing plan so you'll be ready to move on when the time is right.

The book covers:

- **Career management:** A life-long integrated process for both succeeding at your current job and realizing your long-range career goals. The process includes periodic career review, personal planning, marketing, networking and continuing education.
- **SNAPP™ :** The simple, non-technical approach that has demystified project management for successful executives, entrepreneurs and consultants. It shows you how to *See* your career as a project; *Negotiate* with yourself and others exactly what you are trying to do; *Act* by developing a workable plan; *Persist* through successful implementation; and *Praise the Team* throughout. SNAPP™ helps you manage *Your Career, Inc.* by producing both a strategic business plan and a tactical implementation plan.

Although this book talks about reaching your "ideal" career goal, that seldom really happens. The ideal career you now envision will keep changing as you try new things and increase in experience. But the journey should be fun because you'll be challenged and gain increasing confidence in your abilities.

SNAPP™ **shot**

If you don't wake up each morning excited about your day, you're wasting your life.

Who can benefit from reading this book

This book can be used by anyone wanting to know how to get the most from work today while planning for the future. It is for everyone – at any organizational level and in any profession in private, public and non-profit sectors. It is for corporate employees, independent contractors, consultants, temporary employees, entrepreneurs and volunteers. It is for you if you:

- Want to know how to get the most out of your job and career right now.
- Want to know the skills and attitudes most important to today's employers.
- Feel underemployed, face limited growth opportunities, or have been skipped over for promotion.
- Have a tough time going to work in the morning.
- Are in a quandary about whether you're in the right field.
- Are ready to try something new, but are not sure what to do.
- Are just starting out in the business world.
- Are looking for a new job and want to go in with a strong career management strategy.
- Want to maximize your options in any kind of job market.

SNAPP™ shot

You have a choice: manage your career or let it be managed. Taking charge of your own future is the safer and more satisfying place to be.

Why you need this book

This book provides an easy-to-use framework and systematic approach for managing your career from a position of strength. This book:

- Defines the ground rules for the new world of employment so you're not caught unaware.
- Presents the three key success factors that can make you a rising star today while moving you toward your strategic and ideal career goals.
- Outlines a simple, proven technique for ensuring success by making career management a focused project instead of a series of disjointed tasks.
- Contains the career management secrets of leading career counselors, CEOs, corporate training specialists and management consultants to help put you "in the know" and on the fast track.
- Is arranged into modules so you can use it the way you want – as a primer on key concepts in the brave new world of employment, a set of success tips grouped by topic, a step-by-step guide to the career management process, or all of the above.

Perhaps most important, this book helps you answer the question "What do I want to do?" Knowing what you want to do is essential for at least three reasons:

- It provides career focus and direction which will likely lead to a series of successes and ultimate career satisfaction. If you don't know where you want to go, you're unlikely to get there and won't recognize it if you do.
- It allows you to articulate your goals to others. Your network of supporters can help you in your journey only if they know what it is that you want.
- It gives you an edge when you talk with prospective employers about where you fit in the organization. When you can "see it," there's a better chance they can, too.

How to use this book

Chapter 1 describes today's workplace, the key factors for success as an employee and why you must continue to market yourself. The next three chapters cover what it takes to be a valued and enterprising employee, the very first step to success in career management. You must be:

- Entrepreneurial (Chapter 2)
- Excellent (Chapter 3)
- Engaging (Chapter 4).

In Chapter 5 you complete the assessments you began in previous chapters and compile a profile of yourself and your organization that will help you create your career development plan.

Chapters 6 through 11 tell you *how* to embody these key attributes by treating the management of your career as a project. Most people find that things are more likely to get done – and to be done well – when they are well planned and organized as a project. In this section you will be developing several plans and managing several projects at once, each related to the others and all aimed at moving you toward your career goal.

Although this book contains useful templates, self-assessment tools and descriptions of valuable techniques, it does NOT contain all the resources you will need to manage your career. Use it in conjunction with other sources and expert coaching.

Note that to complete the exercises, you can either write directly in the book or access the tools and templates on the Internet at www.careercontrol.com/onlineresources/

Your employer is cheering for you

It may surprise you to know that your employer is probably glad you and other employees are taking the lead in managing your own careers. It is even possible that your company or manager gave you this book. Why is that? For at least three reasons:

- **To give something of value to company employees.** While few organizations can offer employees the virtual guarantee of long-term employment, many progressive companies now assist employees in managing their individual careers. This helps employees develop viable career options that generally lead to greater satisfaction. What's more, it prepares employees to shift more quickly when the inevitable company, industry and marketplace changes occur.

- **To help the company be a learning organization*** in which highly productive employees evolve toward personal mastery, think in terms of the organization's business processes, share the organization's vision and participate in team learning.
- **To retain exceptional employees.** Employees who actively manage their own careers identify and address opportunities to improve their current jobs and typically advance to better positions. Companies expect that this assistance will encourage good people to stay and will thus contribute to building a cadre of leaders. Companies that don't provide this service may risk losing good employees to other companies that do.

Get started today

Getting off to a good start is often the most difficult part. This book can help by providing you with information about what it takes to be successful, self-assessments to help you see where you are now and a structured approach to reaching the goal that you want for the future.

---

* The term "learning organization" is credited to Peter M. Senge, author of *The Fifth Discipline: The Art & Practice of The Learning Organization*, Doubleday/Currency (New York, 1990).

Chapter 1: Prepare for the New Era of Work

 SNAPP™ shot

You must think outside of the box – even when there is no box.

It used to be enough to be employed. If you had a good job at a good company, your employer was expected to provide for your career advancement. Once you convinced the company that you were worth hiring, you were pretty well set for many years to come.

Now that jobs can disappear in the blink of an eye – and companies and even entire industries can fade just as fast – it doesn't mean that much just to be employed. You need an array of skills that will help keep you marketable, within both your company and your industry or specialty. If you show real evidence that you are helping your company create value and make money, your employer will "rehire" you for the next pay period or project by keeping you on the payroll. If you cannot show that you add value, your job may be in serious jeopardy.

This chapter discusses the new corporate model and the implications for individuals who want to effectively manage their careers.

The new workplace

Work isn't what it used to be. The prevailing corporate model – and therefore the way most of us work – changed fundamentally in the last years of the 20th century. The shift has taken corporations:

- From hierarchical to horizontal, or "flat," organization structure – with interdisciplinary teams working independently yet cooperatively.
- From the activity ethic to the performance ethic – assessing employees on the value they have helped create and the results they deliver, not just on the tasks they have completed.
- From bureaucracy to learning organization – helping employees simultaneously increase their effectiveness and satisfaction by learning to manage themselves in a way that meets both ends.
- From employer as parent to employer as partner – calling on employees to take responsibility for their own careers.

- From long-term stable employment to permanent temporary employment that may include consulting, interim assignments and unpaid work.

Under the old corporate model, you were given a job description and a set of relevant objectives. If you met the objectives, you were promoted according to a formal career path. Your job was generally safe unless you did something egregious or your company had to cut back or cease operations. With so much provided, it often didn't make sense for workers to think "outside of the box" and risk shaking things up.

Today, the nature of work can change frequently, downsizing is commonplace, promotions are far from assured and formal career paths are increasingly rare. Workers who simply keep their heads down and follow the rules are no longer the winners; those who keep finding ways to add more value to the enterprise are the ones who prevail and prosper.

Complacency is the enemy.

What the new corporate model means for workers

The rules have changed. Workers are essentially free agents who:

- Will change jobs, on average, every 15 to 18 months and may work for as many as 10 to 20 different employers over the course of a 40- to 50-year career.
- Can no longer be complacent, counting on employers for security and career direction; career management and professional development are their own responsibility.
- Can no longer consider job descriptions (if they exist at all) to be complete lists of what is expected of them; they must become consultants who can identify and address opportunities and solve problems, not just meet stated objectives.
- Can no longer wait for "the boss" to feed them information; they must take the initiative to learn about global business factors and industry, company and professional trends along with the associated essential skills.
- Can no longer rely on solid performance reviews and longevity to push them ahead; they must build an asset base and actively

market themselves in such a way that they maintain good personal relations with a wide range of professional and personal associates.

- Must continually raise their own standards. Each new increment of value demands more creativity and independent thinking. Not only must they now think outside of the box, but sometimes there is no box.

The good news is that the new model offers employees more choices and greater opportunities. Not only can this increase job satisfaction, but according to a Whitehall II Study*, it may also lead to better general health and longer life.

What the new corporate model means for employers

If the new model of employment seems difficult for employees, consider the challenges it has presented for employers due to trends such as:

- The increasing speed of social, economic and commercial change, propelled partly by advancements in all sorts of high technology
- Communications technologies that provide instant access to almost any kind of information, anytime, anywhere
- Deregulation in some industries, exposing once-protected competitors to market forces
- The globalization of markets, increasing the scope of competition from local, regional or national to worldwide
- Ever more sophisticated customers, both wholesale and retail
- The fragmentation of markets into micro-markets, as creative competitors find better ways to target customer needs
- Pressure from investors to increase profitability and productivity, by both adding more value and cutting costs.

The workplace is a new frontier, with both corporate management and employees seeking higher ground. Corporations, used to the old model of employment, must be able to recruit and manage the new kind of employee.

---

* Whitehall II Study, 1985 – 95. Dr. Stephen Stansfield, Department of Epidemiology and Public Health, University College, London.

Success tip 1-1:

THINK OF YOUR EMPLOYER AS YOUR CUSTOMER

As any excellent service provider would, you need to know your customer's needs and buying criteria. Meet those requirements in order to give the company a good reason to "buy from" (or "re-hire") you every day. Strive to exceed expectations. Make yourself indispensable.

Traditional Employer-Employee Relationship	Employer as Customer
Thinks of self as an "employee."	Thinks of self as free agent providing service to a customer – the company.
Security from loyalty to your organization.	Security from delivering what the company needs.
No need to continue education after getting a job.	Life-long learning and re-training.
View of current job as only option.	View of current job as a choice and one of many options.
Commitment to company.	Commitment to performance.
Worker bee: Knows the job and performs it.	Consultant: Knows the industry, the business and the job.
Identification with company and/or job title.	Identification with a team of people, who are all trying to accomplish a set of goals.
Co-dependent: "What can you do for me?"	Independent: "What can I do for you that will also help me?"
Powerless: "What is going to happen to me?"	Empowered: "What can I do to make the right things happen?"
Waits for "them" to decide before taking action.	Makes decisions and takes action based on available facts.

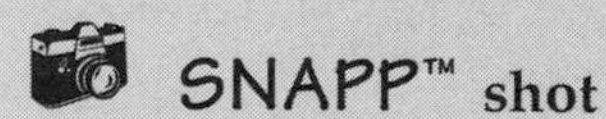

shot

Your only security is the unique set of skills you bring to the marketplace.

The imperative for the enterprising career manager

Now everyone, including the CEO, is in effect a free agent. Every worker must show that he or she creates enough value to deserve to be "rehired" each pay period or review period, or for each project. Not only must everyone work harder, but everyone must learn to operate differently – in a way that gets results in the new era of work.

That means everyone must become enterprising, in terms of both their performance as employees and in terms of their career management.

Key attributes of enterprising employees

An enterprise is a venture that involves courage and energy. To be enterprising means applying courage and energy to your current job, which creates the collateral you need for career management. Enterprising workers have three essential attributes: being **E**ntrepreneurial, **E**xcellent and **E**ngaging, or "E" to the third power – "E^3."

Entrepreneurial: You must manage your job and build your career as an entrepreneur builds a business. After all, your career is a virtual business – *Your Career, Inc.* You must develop strategic career directions and actively follow through on them, adapting your vision to evolving conditions.

As a career entrepreneur, you must package your capabilities into things of value (your own products or services) that meet identified needs (such as your employer's strategic goals) and provide this significant value to your employer or clients (your customers). In order to make your value known, you must devote significant time and energy to a personal marketing program. Like all successful entrepreneurs, you must know the competition. And you cannot do it alone; you'll need to attract a strong support team and create strategic alliances.

There are several types of entrepreneur, as you will learn in Chapter 2. You may be any of these or a powerful combination. Whatever your particular style, you must envision something great, be credible, do everything necessary and appropriate to make it a reality and effectively enlist others in the enterprise.

Excellent: All of your successes will stem from a strong base of excellence in both specific and general areas of expertise. You must be well-versed in general business, your industry and your company. You must know your own job and be skilled in performing it. You must be constantly learning more and gaining new skills.

You probably have several complementary areas of expertise. Each of these may lie in a functional area such as marketing or research and development, in an industry sector like financial services or consumer products, or in a cross-functional specialty such as strategic planning, project management or communications planning. In any case, you must know how to make your knowledge useful and share it effectively with others.

Engaging: You must know how to work with the team and lead people in a way that makes the team a success. You must be respectful of others, courteous and dependable. You need to be approachable, diplomatic and communicative. Listen first, and sell yourself second. You must lead by example.

You may be commanding, charismatic, or collegial, with a dash of compliance when needed. Ideally, you must show a combination of all of these interpersonal styles. In any event, you must get along well with others so they'll want to follow you when it counts.

Lacking top notch E^3 skills and abilities, you're likely to end up in essentially the same old jobs with the same old limitations again and again.

As you develop your E^3 characteristics, however, you are creating value for your current employer while paving the way for your own future career choices. You are becoming an "E^3" employee and career manager.

The E^3 employee and career manager

The attributes of the enterprising employee and career manager can be illustrated like this:

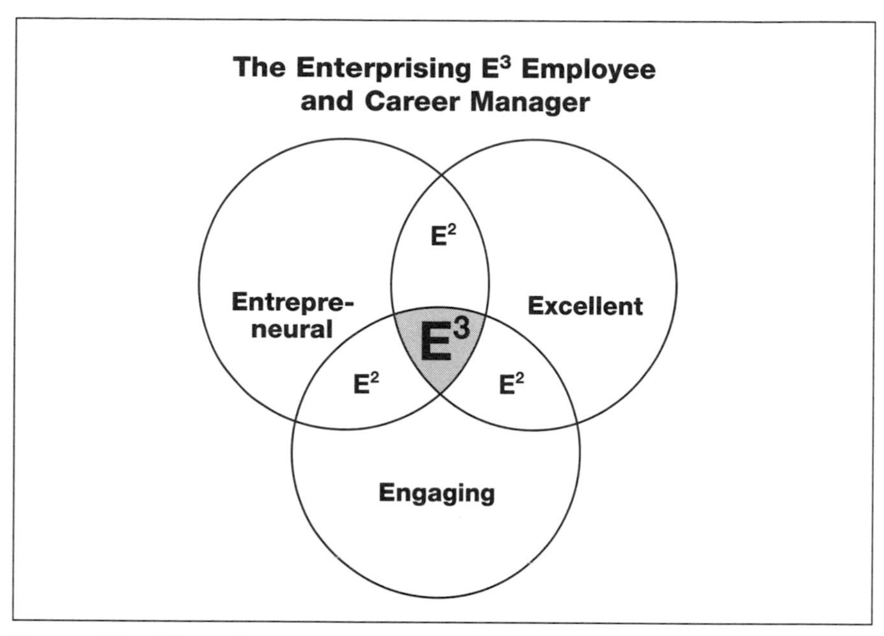

Enterprising E^3 employees and career managers are entrepreneurial, excellent and engaging.

If you find yourself at the intersection of the 3 Es, you are truly enterprising– "**E^3**." As an entrepreneurial employee, you envision creative ways to add value to the enterprise. As an excellent practitioner of one or more business disciplines or functional areas, you support your vision and that of your organization with expertise. And as an engaging person, you enroll others in your vision and add their excellence to your own, in order to achieve tangible results.

While E^3 is the ideal, it is possible to succeed as an E^2. Any combination of strength in two essential attributes increases your value to the organization. Yet you are likely to be limited in the long run by your Achilles heel: the E in which you are relatively weak. Consider the typical consequences of each E^2 combination.

Entrepreneurial x Engaging, but not Excellent: You are good at envisioning how to create something of value and at attracting others to the idea, but you lack the specialized knowledge and skills to understand how to make it work. Consequently, you are dependent on the excellence of others. If you lose access to excellence – if a pivotal expert leaves the team, for example – then your ability to show tangible results is in jeopardy. In the near term, you must depend on your entrepreneurial spirit and engaging personality to secure this essential assistance. In the long term, you will do well to develop your own excellence in key disciplines.

Entrepreneurial x Excellent, but not Engaging: You do high-quality work that is strategically important, but people issues may hamper your efforts. Your work may be perceived as less valuable than it really is simply because people dislike or resent you. In the near term, you may be able to smooth things over by getting an engaging colleague to intercede on your behalf. Some leaders who are perceived as difficult succeed by essentially delegating the job of getting along with others to a more engaging person. If you are at the middle management level or below, however, you don't have that luxury. Lacking strong trust-based relationships with your managers, colleagues and reports, you may be among the first to be downsized. In the long term, you must either improve your people skills or face continual opposition to your excellent ideas and work.

Excellent x Engaging, but not Entrepreneurial: People like to work and socialize with you, but they are apt to overlook what you add because you don't effectively market yourself and your work. Self-promotion is required not only when you interview for a new job, but continuously since you are in effect rehired every day. In the near term, your engaging personality and technical excellence may allow you to keep your job, but you simply cannot get ahead without showing entrepreneurial vision and drive. In the long term, you must identify the distinctive elements of value you can add, package them into desirable projects and end products, enroll others in realizing your vision, and ensure that your successes are visible.

Subsequent chapters of this book will help you identify where your current "E" strengths lie and where you need to concentrate your development efforts.

SNAPP™ shot

Being an E^2 will help you keep the job you have. Being an E^3 will help ensure you have choices about the work you want.

Being an entrepreneurial, excellent and engaging E^3 employee is the basis for your ongoing career progress. As an enterprising employee, you maximize your career options. There will always be employers and customers willing to purchase your services each pay period or project.

At the same time, there are responsibilities associated with being an E³ employee. You must constantly update your skills and abilities, make your actions part of a conscious career development plan and market yourself to others.

For example:

In the early 70s, Lynn was a 20-something high school graduate with no special skills or knowledge and minimal business contacts. She answered a classified ad and was hired for an entry-level position as clerk typist at a mid-sized insurance company, at the time a predominantly male-dominated industry where rising through the ranks was not common. Lynn's first day on the job was inauspicious; she spent part of the morning trying to inconspicuously find the "on" switch to her IBM Selectric typewriter.

She easily mastered the clerk typist position and set out to advance within the organization, laying out a strategic path for her next two career steps. She studied the company, the industry and the general business environment. A "people person," Lynn took a special interest in helping the company's clients. As an E³ employee, she began to achieve her goals, one by one. At each new level of responsibility, Lynn updated her career goals, challenging herself by pushing for training opportunities and volunteering for assignments outside her job description. Her performance was impeccable and her sense of excitement about her work was contagious.

Lynn's reputation grew not only as a reliable expert, but also as an engaging teammate. Her congeniality and grace in effectively dealing with both customers and co-workers at all levels caught the attention of senior management. A series of mentors willingly came forward. In less than two decades, Lynn had progressed to one of the highest levels of senior management in the company.

Although now retired from steady employment, Lynn is still an acknowledged industry expert by scores of colleagues in her vast network. She applies her stellar people skills and entrepreneurial energy to volunteer endeavors, opening opportunities to those less fortunate.

By combining her E³ qualities with a solid career strategy and effective implementation, Lynn was able to achieve her career goal of attaining a position in senior management and her life's goal of doing good deeds in her community.

Success tip 1-2:

HELP YOUR COMPANY BECOME A LEARNING ORGANIZATION

Your role as career manager will be easier if you are part of a "learning organization."

Under the old corporate model, management concentrated largely on controlling what employees did – by limiting information, setting strict targets and monitoring how work was performed.

Under the new "learning organization" model, management directs all employees to learn how best to do their jobs on behalf of the organization. Strict dependence on the lines and boxes in an organization chart is replaced by an emphasis on the *values* that underpin a successfully evolving organization.

The distinctive values of the learning organization are:

- Achieving personal mastery – creating an individual vision that is in alignment with the organization's vision
- Employing mental models – understanding one's personal view of the world
- Communicating shared vision – establishing mutual commitment to a set of values, goals and ideals for the organization
- Facilitating and participating in team learning – creating an environment that promotes the effectiveness of the team.

Companies that succeed in adopting these values find that this mindset can help align the often-conflicting demands of organizational effectiveness and individual job satisfaction, and can increase the organization's capacity for adapting to change. They also report a fuller use of members' abilities and increased motivation.

If your company does not appear to be a learning organization, consider taking the lead in encouraging it. There is abundant information on the Internet and in numerous business texts. SNAPP™ can help you take it on as a project.

Summary

The world of work isn't what it used to be. The key points to remember are:

- There's no such thing as a guaranteed job anymore; the new corporate model requires workers to manage their own careers.
- Employers as well as employees have to navigate new territory. Employers wanting to keep the best employees must provide them with opportunities to develop their skills and abilities.
- To be successful in their current jobs and increase their career options in the future, individuals must develop three important attributes. They must become enterprising employees and career managers who are entrepreneurial, excellent and engaging.
- Being an E^2 helps employees keep the jobs they have. Being an E^3 helps ensure choices about future work.
- No one can rely on past successes. Everyone must constantly update skills and abilities, make their actions part of a conscious career development plan and market themselves to others inside and outside the organization.

Chapters 2 to 4 each explain an "E" and provide a self-assessment tool to help you figure out where you are now. In Chapter 5 you will finalize the self-assessments and complete an organizational assessment. Chapter 6 outlines the SNAPP™ approach you will take to develop your career plan. In Chapters 7 to 11, you will identify your career goals and begin to take steps to achieve them.

Success tip 1-3:

OFFER SOMETHING NEW AND VALUABLE

In all that you do, strive to make both valuable and innovative contributions. Both are key to the success of your organization.

A *valuable* contribution generates or enhances profits, or otherwise creates identifiable benefits that advance the goals of an organization. This requires that you first know the goal and the strategy. Think how your contribution affects the "bottom line."

An *innovative* contribution represents a new solution to a problem, a new response to an existing opportunity or the creation of a new opportunity. Note that you can be innovative by developing new approaches, by applying old approaches in new ways or new environments, or both.

Once you have the valuable and innovative idea, make sure you present it to the right people so that it can be enacted and you receive the credit.

Chapter 2: Be Entrepreneurial

Entrepreneurial x Excellent x Engaging = **E³**

SNAPP™ shot

The company owns your job, but you own your career.

Start Your Own Business: *Your Career, Inc.*

Instead of lamenting new corporate changes, you can use them to your advantage. Instead of waiting for good things to happen *to you*, you can begin to make them happen *for you*.

Managing your career from a position of strength begins with your outlook. From this point on, you must be an entrepreneur, an individual who assumes the risk and management of your own business: *Your Career, Inc.* Vision and drive are what it takes.

This chapter covers the three styles of entrepreneurs and how you can develop entrepreneurial attributes. It also provides a readiness test to help you identify where you are now.

The imperative for entrepreneurship

There are three basic styles of entrepreneur: the Visionary, the Creator and the Achiever. You may be an effective entrepreneur displaying any one of these styles or a powerful combination.

Style	Description	Pluses and Minuses
Visionaries	They *see* opportunities. Their thrills come from creating something distinctive and sharing it with the world. They delegate most details and management to others.	+ They engage the power of people's passion and imagination. Their inspiration and direction add tremendous value. - They may neglect parts of the business that do not interest them. - They often run out of steam between visions.

Style	Description	Pluses and Minuses
Creators	They build new products from existing parts and pieces. The new product or function may be profoundly different from the original.	+ Their practical and flexible approach allows for a quick start. - At times, the product can be an inelegant solution cobbled together. - Their vision may be overwhelmed by the sum of the pieces.
Achievers	They are capable traditional managers with extra vision, passion and drive. Project-focused and end-product oriented, they set goals, analyze tasks and get things done.	+ They know their own limitations and how to enlist help in filling the gaps. - They can be inflexible, and/or find moving on to a new challenge disruptive.

Although in some settings the term "entrepreneur" implies a maverick leader or *prima donna*, in corporate settings most entrepreneurs are team contributors. In ideal teams, there will be visionaries, creators and achievers who work amicably together, combining their talents and compensating for each others' weaknesses.

For example:

Gale Gizmo, Chief Executive Officer of Consolidated Gizmos, Inc., asked three managers with different entrepreneurial styles how they would go about improving manufacturing processes. They responded as follows:

- *The* ***visionary*** *proposed brainstorming sessions with representatives from every department, followed by training so assembly line workers and supervisors could picture what an efficient and effective manufacturing process would look like.*
- *The* ***creator*** *suggested a complete review of the underlying manufacturing strategy. This would be followed by identification of alternative production approaches including both internal and external best practices.**

---

* "Best practices" are good ideas already in use somewhere within the company and/or elsewhere in the industry, and may include applicable techniques from other industries and functions.

- *The **achiever** asked to be made director of manufacturing for a year in order to work the problems out.*

Confused at first, CEO Gizmo soon realized that they were all right and put all three on a task force. Within six months, the manufacturing problems were solved. Each manager had played an important role:

- *The **visionary** designed a two-part program of visioning sessions to help develop a solution and then to assist workers and supervisors in getting familiar with the new approach. Eventually, he was named director of strategic planning.*
- *The **creator** led a review of the manufacturing strategy. The main recommendations were to invest in new systems for efficient production and inventory management and to outsource the less critical manufacturing tasks. Shortly after the project was completed, she accepted an offer to join a prestigious consulting firm. Three years later, she returned to the company as an internal consultant working on strategically important projects.*
- *The **achiever** was made director of manufacturing and successfully implemented the team's recommendations. Ten months after joining the task force, he was promoted to chief operating officer.*

These employees used their entrepreneurial abilities to both get the job done and move their careers forward.

Which of the three entrepreneurial styles best describes your own? It may be predominantly one, or a combination of the three depending on the application. Whatever your style, you must envision something great, effectively market the idea and enlist the help of others.

The demand is immense for people who think and act like entrepreneurs. Opportunities for advancement and finding interesting and rewarding work are greater than ever before – if you know what to do.

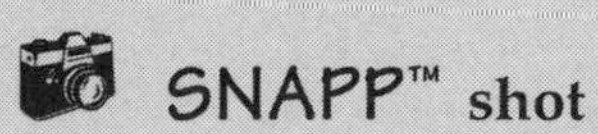

You alone are accountable for your success.

Success tip 2-1:

FORM JOINT VENTURES

A joint venture is an entity formed for a specific purpose and duration between two or more parties. You can form one with your employer.

Your employer and *Your Career, Inc.* are two companies in the same industry with priorities, capabilities and needs that should converge in major areas. Look for areas where your personal vision coincides with your company's mission and goals, and capitalize on that common ground to the benefit of all.

To make it a joint venture and not just an assignment, develop and gain approval for a creative or innovative approach to something that is important to the company. Then take on some strategic as well as tactical responsibility for the venture. Make an investment such as your time, your expertise in bringing about change or your clear thinking abilities.

Example:

An enterprising division manager of a large corporation noticed that numerous representatives from many different business units all were calling on the same customers, often working at cross purposes. Although the business units did not report to him, the division manager took the initiative to call a "summit" of the managers. The group met and created a joint venture to divide up the territory and represent each other's products to the customers. The result was a coordination and synergy of effort that resulted in over $100 million in new business for the corporation. In this joint venture, the division manager further established himself as an entrepreneur, team player and leader. Sales representatives and business units benefited from increased sales, and customers were better served.

Think and act like an entrepreneur

Here are some ways that successful entrepreneurs operate and how you can emulate them in your career.

Key Attributes of Entrepreneurs

What Entrepreneurs Do	What You Can Do
Develop a strategic direction and focus. Entrepreneurs focus on the future in every action they take.	Consider how initiatives fit into the context of the overall economic, industry and corporate picture. Think of your career in terms of a business plan.
Develop new products that customers want. Entrepreneurs can stay in business only as long as their customers are willing to buy.	Think of your employer as a customer. Find ways to provide value and innovative business ideas so your "customer" will continue to purchase your services.
Effectively market their products. Entrepreneurs understand that their products exist solely to make a specific beneficial difference in the lives of customers. They know who their internal and external customers are, what they want and why, and how to attract and serve them.	Identify the following internal and external customers: Current (who are now buying your product), potential (a larger group who may buy your product) and target (on which you will concentrate your efforts). Outline the needs and wants of each type of customer. Develop a plan to attract and retain them.
Take smart chances. Entrepreneurs are willing to take calculated risks that move them along more quickly toward their goals.	Within the bounds of common sense, consider every aspect of your employer's business to be within your realm. Take the initiative to learn other parts of the business by volunteering for committees and projects. Volunteer to be cross-trained in an area that fits your strategic career path.

What Entrepreneurs Do	What You Can Do
Proceed with passion. Entrepreneurs believe in the cause, share the vision and successfully enlist the support of others.	Make sure you are excited about the work that you do and the opportunities that lie ahead. If you are not, escalate plans to move to the next career step. Embrace the challenges. Keep the goal in sight. Go forward with a sense of urgency. Share your vision with others.
Strive to stay ahead of the competition. Entrepreneurs are always looking to differentiate their products.	Avoid being limited by a job description. Remove the phrase, "That's not my job" from your vocabulary. Develop opportunities and solve problems without waiting to be asked. In everyday work, look for opportunities to be creative and take the lead.
Actively promote themselves. Entrepreneurs understand the power of advertising. They get in front of people. They present ideas clearly, persuasively, and appropriately in person and through the media.	Learn and practice these "guerilla marketing" techniques. You can begin on a local level and advance as your comfort level increases. • Network. Build important relationships inside and outside the company. Attend networking events, make connections and ask lots of targeted questions. • With the consent of your employer, give speeches about your area of expertise. (If you're timid, join a group like Toastmasters® to increase skill and confidence.) • Deliver seminars and workshops inside or outside the organization. (If you lack experience, begin by co-delivering with an experienced instructor.)

What Entrepreneurs Do	What You Can Do
	• Write trade journal articles. (If you have little experience, begin with a contribution to the employee newsletter or e-zine.)*
Build credibility. They project credibility by being prepared, decisive, articulate, fair-minded, reasonably optimistic and reliable.	Network to find out how others have built credibility in your field or at your company. Note their outstanding professional and personal characteristics, and strive to embody them yourself. Note their best practices, and employ them yourself.
Own their destinies.	Trust others to assist you (and give credit where due), but remember that you alone are ultimately responsible for your success. Periodically review your goals and ask: What or whom am I waiting for? What can I do to take action now?

You will know you're a successful entrepreneur when your colleagues seek out and act on your ideas and when your customers continue to purchase your product and refer you to others. You will receive company recognition and be considered for promotions.

Understand your readiness to be an entrepreneur

Take a few minutes to assess the extent to which you already are an entrepreneur. Understanding your readiness will help you determine your next steps.

---

* Naturally, you should take care to make your remarks appropriate for your audience and to protect proprietary information. Showing a draft of your speech or article to the company's public relations department is usually a good idea and is sometimes required.

Success tip 2-2:

TAP THE POWER OF YOUR CREDIBILITY

To be a successful entrepreneur, you must be credible. That requires two things: (1) excelling at something and (2) letting other people know. If you lack credibility, why should anyone follow your lead? Try these steps to increasing your credibility.

First you have to excel. Everyone is good at something. Find out your strengths. You can do this through introspection, self-assessment tests, clues from others, past performance reviews, examining your interests, successes and failures – there are any number of ways. Example: You love to solve puzzles of all kinds, and you're very good at it. You wonder how to turn this into an occupation.

Once you know your strengths, capitalize on them. Example: For analytical people, there are dozens of applicable professions. Computer programmers, accountants, doctors, attorneys, psychologists, consultants, writers and teachers all use problem-solving skills. It's a matter of determining where your interests lie.

Train, practice and develop a history of successes. Example: Becoming a computer programmer requires education and practice. Working on successful projects builds experience on which you can trade. Use your experiences to develop a list of "war stories" as validation (see Chapter 10 for examples).

Finally, you must let others know about your excellence. Marketing yourself doesn't mean being overtly boastful. Show rather than tell. Maintain a strong and visible track record. Talk about past projects that were successful; you will shine by association. Establish yourself as an authority by writing articles in trade journals, delivering workshops, giving speeches and volunteering in your field – anything that elevates the visibility of your expertise and contributions. Example: Volunteer to serve on teams and committees where expertise in your area may be needed but in short supply. You become the expert by default.

Personal Assessment Tool: How Entrepreneurial Are You?

Directions: For each statement, circle the number that represents your opinion. Add the numbers, and write the score in the box marked "Entrepreneurial Assessment Total Score." You will need it in Chapter 5.

Note: All questions relate to actions taken within the past year.

1. I have contributed valuable and innovative business-related ideas.

   Do not agree 0 1 2 3 4 5 Completely agree

2. I have contributed important business-related ideas that I persuaded influential people to embrace.

   Do not agree 0 1 2 3 4 5 Completely agree

3. I can name instances where I effectively coordinated the efforts of others in support of a major goal.

   Do not agree 0 1 2 3 4 5 Completely agree

4. I have volunteered for one or more committees or projects outside my immediate unit or scope of job.

   Do not agree 0 1 2 3 4 5 Completely agree

5. I received recognition for taking initiative to solve company-wide problems. Results were measurable, value-added change.

   Do not agree 0 1 2 3 4 5 Completely agree

6. I volunteered to give a speech, write a trade article or deliver a workshop and then carried through.

   Do not agree 0 1 2 3 4 5 Completely agree

7. I regularly attend networking events that result in new contacts that I can comfortably access.

   Do not agree 0 1 2 3 4 5 Completely agree

8. Colleagues seek out and act on my suggestions.

   Do not agree 0 1 2 3 4 5 Completely agree

9. Colleagues refer others to me for advice and direction.

   Do not agree 0 1 2 3 4 5 Completely agree

10. I can see a career path for myself, either inside or outside the company.

    Do not agree 0 1 2 3 4 5 Completely agree

Entrepreneurial Assessment Total Score | |

Interpret your score

Circle the "High," "Medium" or "Low" to correspond with your score.

41 to 50 points. High. Continue to enhance the entrepreneurial skills you have read about in this chapter.

21 to 40 points. Medium. You show some strength. Return to the list and highlight or take note of items you have circled "0," "1" or "2." Make these part of your career development plan for Chapter 9.

0 to 20 points. Low. You need to take action now. Take note of items you have circled "0," "1" or "2." Prioritize two or three. Make these part of your career development plan for Chapter 9.

Summary

To successfully manage your career, you must operate as an entrepreneur who builds and maintains a dynamic business. As a leader you may be a visionary, creator, achiever or a powerful combination. As a career entrepreneur, you will:

- Plan strategically, always thinking two or three career steps ahead.
- Package your capabilities into products or services that meet identified needs, and provide this significant value to your employer or clients.
- Build your personal and professional credibility.
- Devote significant time to developing and executing a personal marketing program.
- Study the competition and strive to stay ahead.
- Take responsibility and proceed with passion.

Once you take steps to become more entrepreneurial, everything changes. You now own your career and accept both the responsibility and the rewards for providing real value to your employer.

Chapter 3: Be Excellent

Entrepreneurial x **Excellent** x Engaging = **E^3**

SNAPP™ **shot**

Being "good enough" is not good enough.

The Yugo. Olestra®. Both of these products represent good, well-marketed ideas, but they never enjoyed widespread acceptance. Why? They didn't live up to their promises.

The product of *Your Career, Inc.* must be excellent. It is the basis for all your marketing claims. This chapter covers the need for excellence in both your work and career management, and what you can do to achieve it. It also provides a self-assessment test to help you identify where you are now.

Excellence is imperative

Your employer is your customer who must be convinced to repurchase or rehire you for each pay period or project. No matter how well your product is packaged, being "good enough" is no longer good enough. If excellence is lacking, your customer will discover that there's little to back up your claims. At best, you will miss the opportunity to have choices about your career; at worst, you will be among the first to go when the company or department must downsize.

To be excellent, you must certainly know your own job and be skilled in performing it. But there is more. You must also be well versed in general business, your industry and your company. Constant learning and growing are perhaps the most important part of being excellent.

That said, being excellent doesn't mean you have to know every last detail or be expert in all aspects of your work. Like everyone else, you have hills and valleys in your skill and knowledge profile. Your "spikes" of higher knowledge or skill may be in the category of general business capabilities, in a functional area such as marketing or research and development, in an industry sector like financial services

Success tip 3-1:

STRIVE FOR BALANCE IN EXPERIENCE

If you aspire to the top ranks of your organization or industry, pursue a path that will provide experience in both line and staff positions.

Line jobs are directly involved with getting and keeping customers. They include production, sales, marketing and customer support units. Line jobs are the ones that make money for the company and get most of the attention. In general, workers in line positions have greater opportunities and more choices.

Staff jobs are indirectly involved with getting and keeping customers. They include lawyers, human resources, research and development, planners, data processing and administration.

Whether your strategy is to advance in line or staff positions, you will need well-rounded experience.

- **If your strategy is to advance quickly to a senior position** in your company, consider a path that moves predominantly through the line with a short rotation in a staff position such as human resources or finance. You'll gain new perspective, skills and knowledge you might otherwise miss.
- **If your intended career is progression through staff positions,** consider at least a short stint in the line business. You'll gain perspective and earn the respect of line business owners whom you'll later serve.

or consumer products, or in a cross-functional specialty such as systems analysis, strategic planning, project management or communications planning. In any case, your knowledge and expertise "product" must be both excellent and useful so that many "customers" are willing to buy it.

Develop your own excellence

Here are some of the attributes of excellent employees and career managers and how you can emulate them.

Attributes of Excellence

What Excellent Employees Do	What You Can Do
Understand general business, the industry and the company. Knowing the big picture, they can put their work in context. These days, few businesses are so narrow and isolated that anyone can succeed by understanding only one industry sector or market.	Make it a priority to understand general business techniques and trends. Find out your company's current and future mission, goals, strategy and environment in which it competes. Collaborate with people from other parts of the company. Get to know people in similar roles in other companies. Keep up with the trends and developments that affect your company's business and industry through study and networking. Engage your manager in a discussion about unit goals that support the strategy.
Take initiative to get the work done no matter what. They are fully and consistently reliable.	Don't limit yourself to what's on your job description (if you have one). Find out what else you're expected to know and do – and exceed the expectation. Find out what's really important to your manager, and deliver it.

What Excellent Employees Do	What You Can Do
	Know what it takes to get your work done properly and appropriately in the real world. Delegate when appropriate.
	Do what you say you'll do on time – and cheerfully – no matter how much extra effort is required.
Know their own skills and abilities.	Discover your strengths. Identify your major interests, values and styles of work. Examine which environments are most conducive to your best work.
	Understand that you don't have to know and do it all yourself. You can enlist the support of other experts.
Develop "general specialties." Many of the people who compete for plum projects and jobs in today's cross-functionally-oriented organizations claim expert status in one or more areas.	To compete, and also to cooperate effectively once you are named to a high-priority team, you must be able to show expertise. Work to develop and enhance functional skills and technical specialties.
	As well as acquiring specialties, work to develop transferable skills such as strategic planning, analysis, communications and project management.
Work effectively in teams of different sizes and in different settings.	Volunteer to lead projects in your area of expertise.
	Volunteer to serve on cross-functional projects and on projects outside your immediate comfort zone.

What Excellent Employees Do	What You Can Do
Follow a rational thought process to guide themselves and others. They demonstrate the ability to make decisions for clear and sound reasons.	Apply a systematic approach such as SNAPP™ to issues and challenges, even when a project is well underway. (See Chapter 6.)
	Educate others in the process to encourage ownership and cooperation.
Effectively multi-task.	Practice working in a structured and disciplined way to help you accomplish more in less time.
	If multi-tasking does not come easily, enroll in a project management and/or time management workshop.

For example:

Perch BeBee, with an impressive resume and record of achievement as director of sales and marketing for a paper products firm, was hired to head the business development effort for a start-up biotech company. Although the scientists and technicians at the new company were aware of Perch's business development skills, they were suspicious of this "outsider." They assumed Perch lacked the capacity to understand and market their products and were cool to his requests for information.

Determined to build credibility, Perch launched into learning mode. He read everything available about the company and the industry, joined and began attending industry association meetings and networked with marketing managers in both competing and non-competing biotech companies. He talked with customers, suppliers and scientists from other firms. In addition to industry-related efforts, Perch joined civic and charitable committees. After making several presentations at professional society meetings on behalf of the company, he noticed that people were beginning to refer to him as an "expert" and a top player in a rapidly growing company.

Inside the company, Perch was able to slowly draw some of the scientists and technicians into discussions by demonstrating his interest and growing knowledge in the industry. Using superior personal and team skills, he finessed invitations to product meetings where at first he merely observed but later began asking pointed questions that helped guide planning and

Success tip 3-2:

MANAGE YOUR MANAGER

Your boss is in the control tower, in a position to decide whether your career takes off, waits in line or slides off the runway into the mud. Here are some ways to keep your manager in your corner, helping you reach your career goals.

- Make your manager's job easier by always doing what you're supposed to be doing – and more. Go the extra mile. As appropriate, coach others in the department.
- Make your manager look good. To do this, you'll need to know what it is that he/she values and wants. If you don't know, ask.
- Don't try to hide the elephant. Never allow your manager to be surprised – particularly with bad news.
- Never fight with your manager; you won't win.
- If you have to approach your manager with a problem, try to provide a plausible solution. If your manager has to solve your problems for you, why pay you?
- Remember that your manager is not your physician, psychological counselor or financial planner. Keep personal problems to yourself.
- Never let your boss make a disastrous mistake. If a crash looks imminent, research the situation and if warranted alert your manager immediately – and usually confidentially. Let the boss take the credit for averting the problem.
- Willingly and graciously accept and support new ideas.
- Initiate ideas for improving customer service, sales, productivity or profitability. Make your case in a businesslike way such as a short written proposal outlining the what, why, who, when, where and how.
- Thank your boss with specific, supportive feedback.
- Train your successor. From day 1 in a new position, make it your goal to prepare someone else who can do your job so you're not so indispensable you can't move on when you want to.

As you take steps to increase your value, be visible but don't flaunt your actions. Perform your work with such excellence that it will be difficult to overlook.

problem resolution. As his credibility grew, Perch was able to help the technical division managers move from their "research and development" mentality to the "for-profit" focus that was needed to keep the company alive.

Although Perch never learned the business sufficiently to become part of his company's biotech product development team (nor did he wish to), he nevertheless was accepted as a valuable player. Profits grew along with Perch's reputation, and he was offered a higher level position in business development at a competing company.

Perch embodies many of the characteristics of an excellent employee and career manager. You'll know you're on the road to excellence when people from all over – inside the company and out – contact you for advice and when you are among the first chosen to lead or participate in high profile projects.

SNAPP™ shot

You must assume responsibility for developing your own skills and abilities.

Personal Assessment Tool:
How Excellent Are You?

Directions: For each statement, circle the number that represents your opinion. Add the numbers, and write the score in the box marked "Excellence Assessment Total Score." You will need it in Chapter 5.

1. I make sure to stay informed about trends and developments in my company and competing companies.

   Do not agree 0 1 2 3 4 5 *Completely agree*

2. People inside the company often request information and my advice about functional areas.

   Do not agree 0 1 2 3 4 5 *Completely agree*

3. People outside the company often request information and my advice about functional areas.

   Do not agree 0 1 2 3 4 5 *Completely agree*

4. People inside or outside the company request information or my advice about areas related to the business in general.

   Do not agree 0 1 2 3 4 5 *Completely agree*

5. My manager and I frequently discuss the company's strategic business goals and how my job contributes.

   Do not agree 0 1 2 3 4 5 Completely agree

6. Currently I am a key member in at least three different projects.

   Do not agree 0 1 2 3 4 5 Completely agree

7. In a recent project, I was able to succinctly explain my thought process in a way that brought new clarity and insight to the group.

   Do not agree 0 1 2 3 4 5 Completely agree

8. Decision-makers ask for my advice on ideas that are potentially valuable or innovative or both.

   Do not agree 0 1 2 3 4 5 Completely agree

9. My projects are completed on time, on budget and to the satisfaction of management.

   Do not agree 0 1 2 3 4 5 Completely agree

10. I am comfortable managing and participating in a number of high-priority projects at one time.

    Do not agree 0 1 2 3 4 5 Completely agree

Excellence Assessment Total Score

Interpret your score

Circle the "High," "Medium" or "Low" to correspond with your score.

41 to 50 points. High. Continue to enhance the excellent skills you have read about in this chapter.

21 to 40 points. Medium. You show some strength. Return to the list and highlight or take note of items you have circled "0," "1" or "2." Make these part of your career development plan for Chapter 9.

0 to 20 points. Low. You need to take action now. Take note of items you have circled "0," "1" or "2." Prioritize two or three. Make these part of your career development plan for Chapter 9.

Summary

Of the 3 Es, increasing your excellence is perhaps the easiest because it generally involves developing skills and acquiring and applying information that is readily available. As an excellent employee and career manager you will:

- Engage in constant learning and growing to develop expertise in functional and technical specialties as well as the specifics of your company and industry.
- Work effectively within teams and as an individual to meet or exceed standards for timeliness, quality and budget control.
- Share your knowledge and expertise with others to improve overall productivity and/or profitability of your organization.

The next chapter provides insight and action items that will help you increase the final characteristic of becoming an E^3 employee and career manager.

Success tip 3-3:

ESTABLISH YOURSELF AS AN EXPERT

To follow through with making speeches and delivering workshops as a way of increasing your credibility, you first need some expertise. Then you need to let others know about it.

Establish your expertise

Search for the under-represented knowledge niche – however small – in which you have some expertise. Perform research, become informed, practice. Talk with people about it. If an identified need doesn't exist in this niche area, try to establish one. This will make you the expert.

Publicize your expertise

Writing articles keeps your name consistently in front of people and creates credibility. Your target audience unconsciously assumes you are important when your name regularly appears on different publications. Almost anything is noteworthy if it is properly pitched. If necessary, start with local publications. For example, volunteer to produce an article for the company newsletter. If you're not a naturally good writer, get some help with crafting the message. Make sure you are credited for each article (i.e., get a byline). Clip and keep copies of your articles. Once you've been in print a few times, your reputation will open doors to more sophisticated publications. As your credibility grows, you are likely to be tapped by other types of media.

You'll know you're an expert when publications and organizations start contacting you for interviews and appearances.

Chapter 4: Be Engaging

Entrepreneurial x Excellent x **Engaging = E³**

SNAPP™ shot

Your skills may get you the job, but your ability to work with others will help you keep it and ensure your success.

With entrepreneurial vision and drive backed up with excellence, you're on your way to being enterprising. But to be a superlative E^3 employee and career manager with influence and choices, you must be expert in finding the right resources to assist you in your efforts and enlisting their cooperation. To achieve that, you must be easy to work with; you must be engaging.

Being engaging doesn't mean being a milquetoast, a pushover or an apple polisher. To the contrary, it requires the utmost in personal and professional integrity. It means self-awareness, self-confidence and self-control. It also means being adaptable and graceful in handling difficult situations.*

Engaging means being approachable, likable and more. To be truly engaging, you must be perceptive in understanding others' visions and goals. At the same time, you must be committed to your own visions and goals, able to communicate them and capable of persuading others to join you. In other words, you must be able to lead. Engaging attributes often determine who is hired or fired, who is passed over and who is promoted. The higher up the ladder you climb, the more vital being engaging becomes.

This chapter covers the styles of engagement and how you can become more engaging. It provides a readiness test to help you identify where you are now.

---

* These qualities are related to those that Daniel Goleman describes in his series of best-selling books on "Emotional Intelligence." See Appendix B for a list of recommendations.

Success tip 4-1:

SHOW, DON'T TELL

You cannot succeed in your career without the support of others. Managers, co-workers and colleagues outside the company must first believe you have the potential. They won't support you if you don't look and act the part. Words won't convince them. You have to demonstrate. In addition to being excellent, engaging and entrepreneurial, here are some tactical ways to show you're capable.

- You will be known by the company you keep. Identify others who are on the upward career path (both inside and outside your company) and concentrate your efforts on developing their friendships. Not only will you gain credibility by association, but you'll learn from their experiences.
- Be respectful and fair with everyone at every level. Give the same courtesy and consideration to the receptionist as you do to the CEO.
- Be genuine and generous with praise and thanks with everyone. It is what great leaders do. You too can look the part.
- Be friendly with everyone, but keep your office-hour conversations on a professional level. Be especially careful what you reveal to others about your personal life. Be careful what highly personal information you allow others to reveal to you. Position yourself as one who is most interested in getting the job done well.
- Create a sense of urgency about the work you do. While maintaining quality standards, beat your deadlines to show that you're capable of greater things. A backlog indicates you need to keep working where you are.
- Don't complain; take action. Enlist others to help.

Engagement is imperative

Engaging employees and career managers exhibit four main styles.

Style	Description	Pluses and Minuses
Charismatic	They pull people toward their vision, leading through inspiration. They solve problems by reframing them (thinking outside of the box).	+ They make people feel significant and fulfilled so they willingly join. - They tend to lose focus periodically and can be self-indulgent.
Commanding	They push people toward their vision of success, leading through power. They solve problems by laying down the law.	+ They make people want to do what it takes to succeed. - They can be autocratic and inflexible.
Collegial	They join the group in moving toward a vision of success, leading by example. They solve problems through negotiation and coaching.	+ They help people enjoy their work. - They may have trouble inspiring a sense of urgency when necessary.
Compliant	They follow someone else's vision of success; they rarely lead. They try to avoid problems.	+ They are liked by people and are often referred to as "salt of the earth." - They often lack the assertiveness to get a fair shake; they can be passive-aggressive.

While these are the predominant styles, most truly enterprising people will apply different approaches in different situations.

Success tip #4-2:

INCREASE YOUR ADAPTABILITY

Being adaptable means having the capacity to change quickly from one idea or situation to another without undue stress. In most work environments, a talent for being adaptable is worth more than an advanced university degree. Some people have it naturally. If adaptability isn't hard wired into your system, there are still some things you can do to develop it.

- Practice discriminating between what you can and cannot control. Act on those things that are under your control; accept those that are not.
- Identify people outside your company who are particularly adaptable. Study what they do.
- Identify adaptable people in your own company. Arrange interviews. Ask targeted questions about how they managed during specific periods of transition and the outcome.

Change is the only constant. Try to view it as your friend instead of your enemy. When you hear that change is in the wind, resist the urge to object. That seldom works in the long run and usually labels you as an obstacle rather than a contributor. Instead, ask about the strategy behind the change. Once you understand, it may be easier to adapt or even lead the charge. Look for the positives, and try to get on board.

For example:

Jarod, the mayor of a city, is a notable example of a career manager who shows an extraordinary balance of engagement styles. Jarod must be commanding when it comes to running an efficient organization that responsibly manages public trust and funds, but he also is charismatic. In situations such as labor disputes and city council disagreements, he favors negotiation and consensus-building over aggressive action. At times he must comply with the directions of the governor. Somehow, he embodies all of these characteristics without detracting from each of them. Jarod's constituents do not doubt this popular mayor's ability to command even though he is charismatic, collegial and even compliant when needed.

Sound difficult? Engaging qualities are not easy to acquire if you don't come by them naturally, but the task is not impossible. One way is to identify effective role models. Watch what they do that's different – ask what it is about them that makes others want to cooperate and follow. Then try to emulate.

Those who achieve such a balance, combined with entrepreneurship and excellence, are able to be truly enterprising. They are aware of their own style of work and interaction and the effect it has on others. They are mature professionals who handle all situations with a cool head and a graceful demeanor. They are team players with effective communication skills. They know both how to lead and how to be led, and when to do each.

SNAPP™ shot

People skills are at the top of employers' lists of hiring criteria.

Take the lead from those who are engaging

Here's what engaging employees and career managers do, and how you can be like them.

Attributes of Engaging Employees and Leaders

What Engaging Employees Do	What You Can Do
Are adaptable. This is number one. People who can easily and gracefully make changes are the most likely to succeed.	If being adaptable doesn't come easily, identify others who roll with the punches. Volunteer to work with them. Study them, interview them and then try to emulate.
Are self aware, self confident and self controlled. They are aware of the image they present to others.	Be aware of the way you work independently and with others. Participate in self-assessment activities and programs (e.g., various 360° evaluations*). If your company doesn't offer career services, acquire them yourself (see Success tip 9-4). Answer the questions openly and honestly, and carefully consider the expert interpretation.
Are courteous and respectful.	Say things like you mean them. Speak clearly. Make appropriate eye contact. Practice excellent table manners. Know the protocol for making introductions. Use polite language. Groom yourself well. Look sharp, even in business casual clothes.

* A 360° profile provides a full-circle view of your abilities and management style by gathering information from various perspectives such as from yourself and from others (e.g., direct reports, boss and peers).

What Engaging Employees Do	What You Can Do
	Practice acceptance of diversity. Study other religions and cultures, read history, and visit other countries. At events, make it a point to talk with people who don't look just like you. Listen to their stories and opinions, and make an effort to relate.
	Handle administrative tasks with grace. Keep up with your e-mail, voice mail, expense accounting and budgeting. Reliably attend and participate in staff meetings. Get to the right places at the right times. Pay attention to expenses as well as revenue.
Are approachable.	When others approach, take time to fully focus and listen, considering the point of view.
	When corrective feedback is offered, thank the contributor. Resist the urge to respond defensively or make excuses.
Are diplomatic.	Most disagreements are semantic. Strive to avoid the quick judgments by listening to and considering other points of view. Resist taking things personally and acting defensively.
	Address possible shortcomings in the team's thinking, rather than verbally attacking individuals with whom you may disagree.
Communicate and influence. They understand that leaders generally are effective communicators.	Articulate your styles of work, your process and the purpose to others when needed.
	If you have to make changes, fully inform and get the agreement of others before acting.

What Engaging Employees Do	What You Can Do
	Be candid but respectful. Use the same principles whether managing down, sideways or up.
Are expert collaborators. They work well with teams, whether leading or participating.	*Teaming* is a necessity in today's business world. Practice to become both an exceptional team leader and a team participant, depending on what's needed. If you're not a natural with teams, follow SNAPP™ to the letter until the process feels comfortable.
Put best people skills into daily practice. They put others at ease because of their consistent and professional manner and approach to individuals and events.	Work on being personable, enthusiastic and cooperative with everyone, even people you don't like. Create a reputation for being fair, fun and faithful to your organization and friends. Take time for people. Strive to be enjoyable. Smile. Laugh. Laugh at yourself. Carry out tasks cheerfully – no excuses and no whining. Be generous. Praise people directly and specifically. Thank people who help you. Apologize when you make a mistake.
Are "heads-up" employees.	Anticipate what the manager wants. If appropriate, do it without being asked. Always make your manager and your team members look good.

What Engaging Employees Do	What You Can Do
Lead by example.	Model the behavior you would like to see in others. Be even more demanding of yourself than others.
Demonstrate maturity. Tolerate disagreement, defuse conflict, and work well under pressure.	Everyone with any responsibility faces problems each day. Work collegially with others to solve them.

You'll know you are engaging when people contact you even when there's no urgent business reason. Although it may seem counterintuitive, people who find you engaging will want to give you advice; because they like you, they take it upon themselves to mentor and coach. Another sign of your engaging nature is that you will hear people quote you and refer to you admiringly when they talk with others. People who find you engaging will likely grant you favors willingly and enthusiastically.

Engaging attributes can be acquired. Begin by assessing your current skills. In Chapter 9 you can identify steps to enhance and make changes.

 **SNAPP™ shot**

If people don't like to be around you, they cannot appreciate your expertise and entrepreneurial nature.

Success tip 4-3:

BECOME A MENTOR

Mentoring in the corporate world describes the practice and process whereby a high-level and experienced manager takes a more junior person under the wing, providing coaching and the right introductions. Most highly successful people have benefited from some level of mentoring.

Characteristics of mentors

Good mentors don't always have to be high-level people. They can be younger – and even less experienced in some areas – than the people they assist. The critical factors are they:

- ➤ Have the capacity to take a personal interest in the growth and development of others
- ➤ Possess skills, knowledge and abilities in specific areas that are needed
- ➤ Are willing and able to share their knowledge and insight
- ➤ Apply a systematic approach, assisting others in defining goals, developing a plan and staying with it.

Consider becoming a mentor to others. There are several reasons to do this:

- ➤ As a humanitarian gesture
- ➤ As a way of developing people in your organization and "building the bench strength" of your corporate team
- ➤ To establish yourself as an expert, poised and caring leader.

Personal Assessment Tool: How Engaging Are You?

Directions: For each statement, circle the number that represents your opinion. Add the numbers, and write the score in the box marked "Engaging Assessment Total Score." You will need it in Chapter 5.

1. I often take time to explain things to teammates.

   Do not agree 0 1 2 3 4 5 *Completely agree*

2. Teammates frequently take the initiative to explain things to me and make other helpful suggestions.

   Do not agree 0 1 2 3 4 5 *Completely agree*

3. I return most of my phone messages and e-mails within 24 hours.

   Do not agree 0 1 2 3 4 5 *Completely agree*

4. I have received feedback from a 360° or career-based personal assessment within the last two years and have acted on the results.

   Do not agree 0 1 2 3 4 5 *Completely agree*

5. I am generally among the first few chosen to join a team.

   Do not agree 0 1 2 3 4 5 *Completely agree*

6. Former colleagues make an effort to stay in touch.

   Do not agree 0 1 2 3 4 5 *Completely agree*

7. I can mediate problems amicably.

   Do not agree 0 1 2 3 4 5 *Completely agree*

8. I hear compliments that colleagues have made about me.

   Do not agree 0 1 2 3 4 5 *Completely agree*

9. I not only tolerate, but appreciate colleagues of different nationalities, races, beliefs, cultures, etc.

   Do not agree 0 1 2 3 4 5 *Completely agree*

10. I am generous with praise and thank-yous to people at all levels of the organization.

    Do not agree 0 1 2 3 4 5 *Completely agree*

Engaging Assessment Total Score | |

Interpret your score

Circle the "High," "Medium" or "Low" to correspond with your score.

41 to 50 points. High. Continue to enhance the engaging skills you have read about in this chapter.

21 to 40 points. Medium. You show some strength. Return to the list and highlight or take note of items you have circled "0," "1" or "2." Make these part of your career development plan for Chapter 9.

0 to 20 points. Low. You need to take action now. Take note of items you have circled "0," "1" or "2." Prioritize two or three. Make these part of your career development plan for Chapter 9.

Summary

Of the three Es, the quality of being engaging may be the most important factor in your success. If you aren't naturally engaging, you can work to develop it. You may be commanding, charismatic, collegial or compliant. Ideally, you will show a combination of all these interpersonal styles. As an engaging employee and career manager, you must:

- Be adaptable.
- Know how to work with the team and lead people in a way that makes the team a success.
- Be respectful of others, courteous and dependable.
- Be approachable, diplomatic, communicative and helpful.

Now you know about the era of today's workplace and what it takes to be an enterprising E^3 employee. You have gathered some data about yourself. Before you're ready to build and follow a career development plan, however, there is some additional data gathering and interpretation to be performed. In the next chapter, you assess the final elements affecting your career in the near term: your working environment and your own propensity to make change.

Chapter 5: Prepare to Take Action

Are you sufficiently entrepreneurial, excellent and engaging? If yes, you're highly marketable and at least one step ahead of the crowd; keep going. If you're lacking in one or more Es, you'll need to work harder, but there's still time.

In this chapter you will compile the scores from the three "E" assessments and determine your E^3 rating. You will perform three more short assessments to determine the readiness of your organization to support you and your own readiness to move forward.

The E^3 readiness factor

Now it's time to find out how you rate overall in terms of the three Es.

Personal Assessment Summary

Directions: Transfer your numeric scores from the self-assessments at the ends of Chapters 2, 3 and 4 into the "Your scores" column of the matrix below. Then, add all the scores to create the Total, and check the Interpretation.

	Total points possible	Your scores
Entrepreneurial	50	
Excellent	50	
Engaging	50	
Total	150	

Interpret your score:

- **123 to 150 points. High.** You are an enterprising employee. Your main need now is to develop your career plan so that your next career step is all it can be. Don't neglect the Es, though. You can always enhance your entrepreneurial abilities, your excellence and your already engaging people skills by working on your adaptability – another key to staying on top of the Es. (See Success tip 4-2.)

- **63 to 122 points. Medium.** You are on your way to becoming enterprising, but you need to fill a few gaps first. Use the information in Chapters 2, 3 and 4 and the self-assessment questions as a starting point. In Chapter 9, you will make a plan for filling the gaps.
- **0 to 62 points. Low.** You probably are not ready to shape your own career in a fully enterprising way. You need to identify the gaps that are keeping you from being entrepreneurial, excellent, and engaging. Use the information in Chapters 2, 3 and 4 and the self-assessment questions as a starting point. In Chapter 9, you will make a plan for filling the gaps.

If you have a high score (41 to 50) in each of the three attributes, you can begin to develop a marketing plan around your E^3 profile. If you're weak in one or more of the Es, you can take steps to fill the gaps. You'll learn how to do both in Chapters 7 to 11.

The employer readiness factor

Now you need to make sure the time is right.

It isn't enough for you alone to be enterprising. You work within an organization that must also be ready. What's more, as an employee of a specific department, you are working for an organization within an organization.

If your company and/or the employees in your department are not fully on board with the learning organization model, your E^3 qualities may be under appreciated – or possibly even detrimental to your job. Your company and the people with whom you work have the power to amplify or narrow your career aspirations. You will need to account for this in your career development strategy as you work through the remainder of this book.

Use the following tools to assess the readiness of (a) your company and (b) your department.

A. Company Readiness Assessment

Directions: For each statement, circle the number that represents your opinion. Add the numbers, and write the score in the box marked "Company Readiness Total Score."

1. My company practices an open-door policy that encourages employees at all levels to approach senior management to discuss ideas.

   Do not agree 0 1 2 3 4 5 Completely agree

2. My employer encourages trust.

   Do not agree 0 1 2 3 4 5 Completely agree

3. My company encourages constructive dialogue about company rules and strategy.

   Do not agree 0 1 2 3 4 5 Completely agree

4. My company provides leadership training for employees at my level.

   Do not agree 0 1 2 3 4 5 Completely agree

5. My company is of sufficient size and diversity that I have opportunities to move from one department to another.

   Do not agree 0 1 2 3 4 5 Completely agree

Company Readiness Total Score

Scoring

21 to 25 points. High. Your company appears to subscribe to the new corporate model that recognizes and encourages E^3 employees.

11 to 20 points. Medium. Your company may be in transition between either more or less of a learning organization.

0 to 10 points. Low. It appears your company lacks the fundamentals of a learning organization.

B. Department Readiness Assessment

Directions: For each statement, circle the number that represents your opinion. Add the numbers, and write the score in the box marked "Department Readiness Total Score."

1. My supervisor and I have had a recent conversation focusing on my career progression.

   Do not agree 0 1 2 3 4 5 *Completely agree*

2. My immediate supervisor has demonstrated interest in my career progression.

   Do not agree 0 1 2 3 4 5 *Completely agree*

3. There are other positions I can advance to within my area/department.

   Do not agree 0 1 2 3 4 5 *Completely agree*

4. My manager treats employees as partners rather than overhead.

   Do not agree 0 1 2 3 4 5 *Completely agree*

5. Among my co-workers, there is a spirit of collaboration rather than competition.

   Do not agree 0 1 2 3 4 5 *Completely agree*

Department Readiness Total Score [ ]

Scoring

21 to 25 points. High. Your department/supervisor appears to subscribe to the new corporate model that recognizes and encourages E^3 employees.

11 to 20 points. Medium. Your department/supervisor may be in transition, either slow or rapid.

0 - 10 points. Low. It appears your department/supervisor may not be supportive of your career plans.

Interpretation of company/ department readiness

The following matrix indicates possible next actions depending on the readiness of your company and department.

Note that the matrix has boxes only for "High" and "Low." If one or both of the scores on your company and department readiness result in "medium" scores, this means your situation may be in transition, either slow or rapid. Be attuned to movement in either direction. Do what you can to move it to the "high" side. Initiate a discussion with your supervisor. Let him/her know your aspirations, and note the reaction and results. This will help you decide whether there is a future for you in this company and department.

The readiness of your company and the people in your immediate department will influence your career plans and the next steps you take.

Company and Department Readiness

	Low *Department is NOT ready for E³ employees*	**High** *Department is ready for E³ employees*
High *Company is ready for E³ employees*	**Right company, wrong department** You work for a learning organization, but the people in your department don't support the same values. Consider career opportunities outside this department.	**Right place at right time** Both your company and the people you regularly work with are likely to be supportive of your career development. Work to enhance your E³ qualities, develop your career plan, and you're on your way!
Low *Company is NOT ready for E³ employees*	**Wrong company, wrong department** This company does not appear to be a good fit long-term. Consider a move to a company that will support you in your career goals.	**Wrong company, right department** If you're learning and growing within your department, you may want to stay where you are until you achieve your growth goals. Unless the company makes a shift, however, you'll likely need to leave.

Now you know where you stand in terms of your E³ strengths and weaknesses. You also have identified your company's and department's degree of readiness.

There is one last readiness assessment. It is your own willingness to change and take action. Lacking the will, you cannot be successful.

C. Personal Change Readiness Factor

Directions: For each statement, circle the number that represents your opinion. Add the numbers, and write the score in the box marked "My Change Readiness Total Score."

1. I believe that I (rather than the company) am responsible for my career and my future.

   Do not agree 0 1 2 3 4 5 Completely agree

2. In order to make the change I want, I am prepared to spend free time in activities such as networking and training and to operate outside my comfort zone with activities such as delivering speeches and workshops in my area of expertise.

   Do not agree 0 1 2 3 4 5 Completely agree

3. In order to make the change I want, I am prepared to spend my own money on activities such as networking and training.

   Do not agree 0 1 2 3 4 5 Completely agree

4. I see other jobs in my company or field that I want to try.

   Do not agree 0 1 2 3 4 5 Completely agree

5. In order to make the change I want, I am willing to move to a different company or change careers.

   Do not agree 0 1 2 3 4 5 Completely agree

My Change Readiness Total Score [ ]

Scoring

21 to 25 points. High. You appear to be highly motivated to manage your career.

11 to 20 points. Medium. You appear to be moving in the direction of initiating change.

0 to 10 points. Low. It appears you are not ready to make a commitment to change. Put this book on the shelf. Return to it when you feel more ready.

Summary

Now roll together the results of all the assessments.

All Assessments Summary

Directions: Complete the following table by writing the result ("High," "Medium" or "Low") next to each of the assessments.

	High / Medium / Low
Three Es	
Company	
Department	
Personal readiness	

Align your readiness assessments

Use the following table to help you determine your career options depending on your company, department and self-readiness. Any "medium" range assessments indicate that the entity is in transition; you must be the judge of whether it is moving toward "high" or "low."

Ready?			Suggested Interpretation
Company	Dept.	Self	
Low	Low	High	1. You can't fundamentally change the company. Consider other potential employers before long.
High	Low	High	2. You could be limited by the department you're in, but don't give up on the company until you've investigated other areas.
Low	High	High	3. Enterprising opportunities are limited to your department. Make the most of your current opportunities, while investigating other potential employers.
High	High	High	4. Congratulations! You are in a good position to further develop your 3 Es. Create your career development plan. Think two or three steps ahead.

Align readiness with E³ attributes

There is one last question before you begin your career development plan. How has your career been progressing to date? Is it moving along at the clip you'd like, or is it too slow to suit you?

If you have completed the three "E" assessments with flying colors (as a "high medium" or "high") and your department and company are "ready" but you're feeling undervalued or are being passed over for promotions, the results of one or more of the assessments may be questionable. Try to validate the results by enlisting the help of two or more trusted current and former colleagues (no family members) who know your work style. Do the following:

- Ask them to review the "Attributes of . . . " sections of Chapters 2, 3 and 4 and give you feedback. They can use the entries as talking points.
- Ask them to make specific observations about your qualities and characteristics, commenting on both your strengths and your weaknesses.
- Listen to their comments without responding verbally. (If your colleagues sense even the slightest defensiveness, they are likely to curtail their honest reports and you will be the loser.)
- Ask them to critique your answers to the Company and Department Readiness questions to see if they agree with your assessment.
- At the end, thank them sincerely for their help.
- Adjust your scores as indicated, and be guided by colleagues' feedback.

The next chapter outlines the approach you'll take in acting on this information as you move toward success in career management.

Chapter 6: Make Career Management a Project

 SNAPP™ shot

You are the project manager of your career.

Successful people all have one thing in common. Instead of letting things happen *to* them, they make the right things happen *for* them. They set viable goals and then apply a structured and disciplined approach to meeting them. That may sound onerous, but it needn't be. It involves simple project management.

People often associate project management with computer systems and technology, but it's not really that technical or mysterious. Project management merely lays out a structured path to meeting and exceeding goals. In fact, project management has been around since ancient times. The Vikings used it to explore new worlds. The Romans used it to build roads, temples and aqueducts.

What is project management?

Project management is the active control that enterprising individuals use to get things done better and faster, through forethought, planning and a lot of follow-through. Project management can be successfully applied to everything from managing children to managing a political campaign. If you have used project management techniques in your work, you will immediately understand the link to career management. If you have never thought of yourself as a "project person," that is about to change.

What is SNAPP™?

SNAPP™ is the practical, "bare bones" of project management. Once you learn it, you are likely to use SNAPP™ to tackle all challenges coming your way.

SNAPP™ demystifies project management. Two stages, planning and implementation, incorporate five non-technical and easy-to-remember steps. The SNAPP™ framework, with key questions to ask, appears on page 63.

Success tip 6-1:

APPLY KEY SNAPP™ PRINCIPLES

Like many processes, SNAPP™ has its own key terms and principles. You can apply these to any project you undertake, professional or personal.

- **Embrace ownership.** Feelings of responsibility and accountability describe ownership. Success in career management will depend on your commitment to owning the challenge and the outcome.
- **Consider your stakeholders.** People who can advance or hinder your career or who will be affected by your progress are your stakeholders. They include family, friends and colleagues.
- **Employ the team.** Few things in life – either business or personal – are accomplished successfully without team support. Your career management team can include managers, mentors, consultants, friends, colleagues and family members.
- **Commit goals to paper.** Putting things in writing adds emphasis to any project. It also provides a useful reference. Make and follow an action plan – your most important piece of written documentation. Use checklists. In addition to helping you keep score, action plans can also help you "de-stress" because you will have fewer things to commit to memory.

The SNAPP™ letters stand for:

Planning stage

S = See It. You must know where you're going so you'll know it when you get there. S = See It entails setting *what* your goal will be, establishing *why* you want it and considering *who* will benefit.

N = Negotiate It. Once you know your goal, you analyze it from every angle and work out all the details – with yourself and others. This includes the scope, resources, risk, budget, assumptions and contingency plans.

A = Act on It. Next, you draw up a detailed action plan, assign accountabilities, get agreement from your team members and begin to carry out the tasks.

Implementation stage

P = Persist. Once the S-N-A is set, persistence is the make-or-break step that keeps you on track and moving in the right direction. You actively monitor your progress, stay focused on the goal, network and remain upbeat through it all.

P = Praise the Team. No one completes a project alone. The key to success is properly positioning the project so others will want to participate. Throughout the project, the successful manager praises the team. At the end, there's a celebration.

SNAPP™ works as well for career management as it does for every other endeavor. Using SNAPP™ increases the odds you'll take the next right step on the road to a satisfying career. By failing to take a strategic and structured approach, you risk languishing in your job or heading off in the wrong direction.

For example:

Eager for almost any good-paying job to support the family after completing his MBA, Telly accepted the position of systems analyst within a technical division of a major bank. Although he initially enjoyed the work, after two years he became bored and began to wonder, "What else is there?" He remembered that his intent when entering graduate school was to pursue a career in credit management. In the meantime, he and his wife had traveled abroad and were dreaming of living and working in a foreign country.

One of the divisions of the bank was in the business of developing products and services for large multinational companies. Telly began networking with managers of the multinational division, and before long he was named systems manager. During the two years in this role, Telly continued to network. He talked with officers in the international division, letting them know of his ambition to become a credit officer and work abroad. He volunteered for cross-functional teams that served both multinational and international divisions. In his free time, he took a foreign language course to further demonstrate his commitment.

The strategy worked. Telly accepted a position as international division credit trainee, with no loss of grade or pay. Within two years, Telly was posted to Asia where he and the family spent four years that they still describe as one of the best periods of their lives.

Telly is an enterprising employee who used his project management skills to set a career strategy, develop and follow a plan, use a network of resources and stay focused to reach the goal.

Apply SNAPP™

Success in most areas requires discipline, focus, training and practice in a supportive environment. The next five chapters lead you through a structured project management approach to career management that includes all these elements. Chapters 7, 8 and 9 cover the elements of the planning stage. Chapters 10 and 11 outline the *how-to* of self-development, marketing and team management that will help you achieve your career goals.

Learning and practicing the steps will also help you increase your abilities as an E^3 employee. You can SNAPP™ your next right career step and any of the attributes you identified in the self-assessments as areas for development and enhancement.

The SNAPP™ steps as they apply to career management appear on the following page.

S	N	A	P	P™

Career Management is a SNAPP™

Planning Stage

S = See It

1. What does it look like when I've got it right?
2. Why do I want this?
3. Who else cares and why?
4. What do I have to offer?
5. What knowledge, skills and abilities will I need?

N = Negotiate It

1. What is the scope of the effort?
2. What are the assumptions?
3. Who will help?
4. What can change or go wrong?
5. What are the financial implications?

A = Act on It

1. What's the action plan?
2. Who is accountable?
3. Who will support it?

Implementation Stage

P = Persist

1. Mind the details and keep score.
2. Recruit and retain your team.
3. Develop and maintain a communications package.
4. Stay focused.
5. Play the role of the position you seek.

P = Praise the Team

1. Make it a plus.
2. Say thank you.
3. Close and celebrate.

Success tip 6-2:

BECOME AN ENTERPRISING PROJECT MANAGER

Effective project managers have skill sets of their own. Regardless of the assignment, to be a truly enterprising project manager you must:

- **Focus on the goal.** Regardless of the distractions, you must be single-minded and persistent in attaining the goal.
- **Make sound decisions.** Make necessary and timely decisions within your authority level.
- **Embrace ownership.** You must feel responsible and accountable for the success or failure of the project, as though you were protecting some valuable object.
- **Enjoy people management.** Project management is people management.
- **Lead.** The team looks to you. You must model the behavior you want to see in others, and give the glory to the team. Lead by example and manage by influence.
- **Communicate.** Listen as well as speak. Negotiate so everyone wins something.
- **Be adaptable.** You must value diversity of thought and skill and tolerate ambiguity when necessary. You must champion positive change.

Chapter 7:
S = See It

SNAPP™ shot

Don't play checkers with your career; play chess.

S = See It is the first step in the planning stage that lays the foundation for your career moves, in both the long run and the short. You will always be thinking two to three steps ahead while simultaneously enhancing your "E" attributes. Once goals are established, you will revisit them regularly throughout your career management effort.

The three planning stage steps are, in order:

S = See It

N = Negotiate It

A = Act on It

A case example, which runs throughout the remaining chapters, will help to illustrate the process.

♣ Meet Ellee, E^3 employee

In your journey through SNAPP™ you can follow the progress of an enterprising individual named "Ellee." Although Ellee and all the details are fictional, her character is based on a composite of real-life professionals, and her experiences are typical of others who have used SNAPP™ to effectively manage their careers. The Ellee model demonstrates how the SNAPP™ template can be used as a career development tool for both short-term and long-term goals.

Ellee is a thirty-something marketing professional with a life's mission of achieving sufficient career success that she can serve as a model for others.

Fifteen years ago, shortly after her university graduation with degrees in marketing and communications, Ellee joined a small, privately owned company where she served in a variety of sales, marketing and advertising roles.

Five years ago, ambitious to continue improving her skills and increasing her influence in a marketing role, she joined the global telecommunications giant Tele-tele Corporation (T-TC). To get her foot in the door, she accepted a position as a marketing projects coordinator. Thanks to her hard work, many sterling E^3 attributes and just plain being-in-the-right-place-at-the-right-time, Ellee advanced quickly through several positions to her current role as Senior Marketing Manager for Domestic Products Division, a middle management position with a staff of five direct reports.

Ellee enjoys working for T-TC. She feels fairly compensated in terms of salary and benefits, and she has built many friendships. She has been recognized for her work with service awards and regular bonuses, and she is satisfied that T-TC supports her pursuit of growing responsibility and influence. Ellee recognizes her good luck in working for both a company and a manager that support a learning organization mentality.

In her private life, Ellee is a single mother with elementary school twins. For Ellee, another advantage of T-TC employment is a degree of flexibility in managing her work schedule. Most days, she can arrange to spend time with her young children during late afternoon and early evening.

With two years of experience in her current position, Ellee recognizes oncoming boredom as a sign that she needs to take her next career step. She has completed the readiness assessments appearing in this book. She scored high in both the entrepreneurial and excellence scales. Being honest, Ellee recognizes that her shortcomings in people skills sometimes get in the way of her effectiveness. She resolves to work on becoming more engaging while pursuing her long- and short-term career goals.

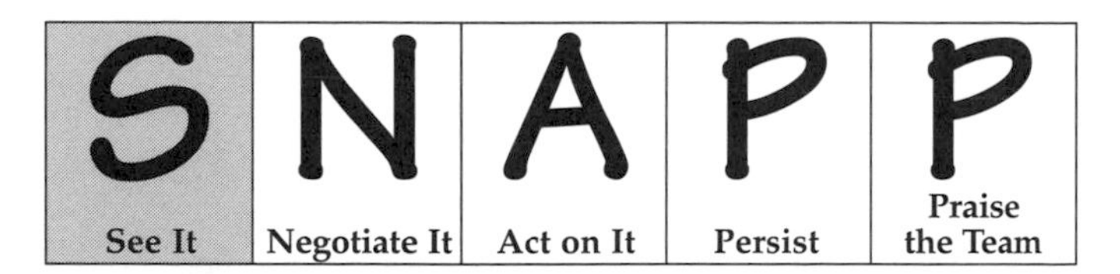

S = See It

SNAPP™ shot

If you don't know your career goal, any next step will do.

In the S = See It step, you take a high-level view of where you want to be in the long and near terms, where you are now and what it will take to fill the gaps.

In the very long term, you may have a vague idea about your "ideal career." That's what you envision now as the pinnacle, the point at which you have achieved everything in your career game plan and are making the difference you want to make. Keeping that in mind, the S = See It step helps you visualize at least three goals toward which you'll be simultaneously moving:

- **Strategic career:** Because the business world changes so rapidly and because people so often change their minds along the way, three to five years is about as "strategic" as most people can plan. Your strategic career generally is two to three steps away from where you are now.
- **Near-term, "next right career step:"** This job should fit into your strategic career plan. You may reach it within the next four to six months depending on any number of factors.
- **E^3 goals:** In order to succeed in reaching your current intermediate and ultimate career goals, you must continually develop and enhance the skills and abilities that make you a truly enterprising, E^3 employee.

In S = See It, you document your answers to the following questions:

1. What does it look like when I've got it right?
2. Why do I want this?
3. Who else cares and why?
4. What do I have to offer?
5. What knowledge, skills and abilities will I need?

Success tip 7-1:

FIND OUT WHAT MOTIVATES YOU

Discover what charges your batteries on a daily basis. Be aware of this as you consider career possibilities. The list below contains some common work values. Place a ✔ by those that are the most important to you; then prioritize them. Consider whether they are aligned with your strategic and next right step career goals.

- Autonomy
- Challenging work
- Change and variety
- Competition
- Creative opportunities
- Defined boundaries
- Details
- Fast-paced work
- Fiscal responsibility
- Flexible hours
- Friendships
- Helping others
- Increased responsibility
- Interesting and intelligent co-workers
- Leadership opportunities
- Learning environment
- Money
- Outdoor work
- Pleasant aesthetics of work environment
- Precision work
- Project work
- Public contact
- Risk, adventure
- Sense of community
- Team work
- Travel
- Work with ideas
- Work with people

1. What does it look like when I've got it right?

This is the most powerful question in all of SNAPP™. Before you begin any planning, you must be able to clearly imagine your strategic career when you're "there"– where you are physically, whom you're with, what activities you're performing, what you're contributing and how others are reacting. What's more, you should be able to articulate it in 25 words or less. Let your career dreams flow.

Consider the parameters of your strategic career:

- **The type of organization.** Will it be a big corporation? A mid-sized company? A small, family-owned business? A high-potential startup? A non-profit? What are the significant differences in the work environment, organizational culture, goals and available opportunities?

  Will you have your own business? Even if you'll be self-employed, you will be creating an organization with a life of its own. Consider how your enterprise will be shaped by your own personal goals and style and how you will engineer that.
- **The business area.** Will you be a specialist, staying within a specific industry and/or a specific function such as technical instruments salesperson or contracts attorney? Or will you operate as a generalist in a cross-functional specialty such as corporate communications or international relations? Don't limit yourself. As discussed in Chapter 3, everyone has strengths and areas of higher knowledge and skill.

In your analysis, don't lose sight of the things that you like and don't like to do. You may want to list them in separate columns and allow them to figure heavily into your career plan. Sometimes you have to take interim career steps that involve tasks and jobs not to your liking, but make it your goal to minimize time doing things you actively dislike. Even when you're good at them (e.g., grant proposal writing or architectural drafting), in the long term you will not be successful at tasks and jobs you don't enjoy.

➠ SNAPP™ it!*

Complete the following tables – in pencil. It's important to record your plans so you can refer to and refine them.

Each of the tables calls for two visions: your "strategic career" and your "next right career step." Complete both. In each case, add criteria specific to your situation.

Complete Table 7-a if your goal is to be employed by a company. Complete Table 7-b if your goal is to be self-employed, participate in a partnership/joint venture or devote yourself to volunteer endeavors. If you're not yet sure which you want, fill out both. Everyone should complete Table 7-c: "My lifestyle."

Table 7-a If I will be employed by a company:

	Strategic career goal	Next right career step
What work will I be doing (same or new functional area)?		
Specialist or generalist?		
What industry?		
What size company?		
Public or private company?		
With whom will I be working?		
Other important criteria.		

* **Note:** Throughout the remainder of the book, you will see paragraphs marked "SNAPP™ it!" This is your invitation to perform a task that will lead you toward your next right step and career goal.

Table 7-b If I will be self-employed or a consultant, in a partnership, joint venture or volunteer role:

	Strategic career goal	Next right career step
What will the industry be?		
Will it be profit or non-profit?		
What will the product/service be?		
What work will I be doing?		
Who will my customers be?		
Who will my partner(s), if any, be?		
Other important criteria.		

Table 7-c My lifestyle:

	Strategic career goal	Next right career step
Where will I be living?		
Will I be renting or owning a home?		
With whom will I be living?		
Earnings and benefits needed.		
Perks wanted.		
Work hours per week.		
Off-work activities.		
Other important criteria.		

Success tip 7-2:

LOOK FOR SHARED VALUES

Shared values between you and the company are essential to an ongoing and satisfying relationship. The topic bears investigation and consideration when targeting companies and pursuing jobs. By some estimates, nearly half of all dissatisfaction with jobs is due to lack of shared values.

You can gain insight into a company's values by reading the annual report or visiting the company's Web site. Consider the mission statement. Does it match your values? If community service is important to you, is there any statement about such commitment? Are statements matched by financial contributions? Do the actions of your company and immediate manager match your beliefs about treating people with respect and dignity?

Company values should also be evident at the department level. Does the department's commitment to quality match yours? If you like to volunteer, will your department manager support your commitments and even allow time off?

An obvious clash of values is a red flag that your career plans may be taking a detour.

♣ **Ellee sets her strategic career and next right career step goals.**

In the very long term, perhaps after the twins have graduated from college, Ellee plans to run her own business. Her career mission is to attain sufficient recognition as a functional expert and business owner that she will serve as a role model and mentor to other women in reaching their highest career goals. For at least the next five to ten years, however, Ellee thinks she needs the stability of a regular paycheck.

After considering her likes and dislikes and various possibilities, Ellee thinks she has several career options. One is to continue on the current marketing path. Other possibilities are corporate communications and a specialty in project management.

She also determines that there are a number of sound professional and personal reasons for staying with T-TC in the near future. As she considers the T-TC career opportunities, she decides that the position of Director of Marketing for Global Products Division will be her strategic career target. On a professional level, the position offers potential for influence in the direction and profitability of T-TC. It also offers the opportunity for positive recognition as a powerful executive if she does the job well. This will provide an excellent springboard for almost any career path she decides to take.

As for her lifestyle, Ellee hopes that additional salary from new career steps will allow her to purchase a larger home and begin saving for the twins' college education. In any new job, she needs roughly the same flexible hours that she now enjoys. As a pastime, Ellee belongs to a Toastmasters® club as well as a speakers bureau. She likes giving humorous speeches and often donates her services at charity events. For her required participation at the children's private school, Ellee offers career counseling to high school juniors and seniors. A flexible schedule and the ongoing support of T-TC in participating in community activities are key factors in her decision to stay at this company.

Given her current strengths and experience, Ellee thinks she will need at least two more steps before reaching director level of the Global Products Division, but if she systematically manages the process, the position is a viable destination. She considers several options for her next right career step:

1. *Enriching her current job by taking on more entrepreneurial marketing projects, with the approval of her supportive manager.*
2. *Transferring to the Global Products Division as a project manager so she can learn the organization through leadership of cross-functional teams.*
3. *Transferring to the Global Products Division as manager for one of the products.*

Ellee thinks that her best next interim step will be the third option. That position will provide an entry into the division while teaching her the ins and outs of product development – a skill that will serve her well in her strategic career.

2. Why do I want this?

If you are to be successful, both your strategic career goal and your next right career step should direct you toward fulfilling your basic emotional, financial, social and physical needs. Here's why.

Emotional. Ideally, your interests and skills should overlap, so that the work you perform is satisfying and fills a higher need than merely "earning a living." If you're in the right place, you should wake up in the morning eager to get to work. When people ask, "What do you do?" you should be proud to tell them.

Financial. You need to comfortably support yourself and possibly others. Your compensation should also accommodate your financial planning strategy and charitable giving. Ask yourself, "If I earn this amount, will I feel I'm sufficiently and fairly compensated?"

Social. Like people, organizations have unique "personalities" and value systems. You're likely to be most satisfied when your personality and values match the culture of the department and the organization. For example, if you like a lot of structure, you may be uncomfortable working in a loosely managed environment.

Physical. You want to work in an environment that fits your lifestyle and physical needs. Consider workplace amenities (old/new, light/dark, high energy/quiet, open/closed office), urban or suburban location and amount of indoors or outdoors work. Consider any special or unique ergonomic needs.

➡ SNAPP™ it!

Document *why* you feel this strategic career and the next step are the right ones. In the matrix that follows, indicate whether each of the four factors supports your identified strategic career goal and your next right career step choices. Use either the scale of 1 to 5 (5 = **S**trongly **A**gree, 1 = **S**trongly **D**isagree), or a narrative approach.

Table 7-d Why I want this:

	Strategic career goal	Next right career step
	SD ➡ SA	SD ➡ SA
Emotional: I will enjoy this work and be proud to talk about it.	1 2 3 4 5	1 2 3 4 5
Financial: This work will provide sufficient compensation.	1 2 3 4 5	1 2 3 4 5
Social: I will share values with the organization.	1 2 3 4 5	1 2 3 4 5
Physical: The environment will suit my work style.	1 2 3 4 5	1 2 3 4 5

Now review your scores. Are there are any that are 1 or 2? If yes, you may want to reconsider your career or next right career step goals.

 **Ellee revisits her goals.**

Table 7-d Why I want this:

	Strategic career goal: Director of Marketing	*Next right career step: Product Manager*
Emotional:	*Help lead T-TC in quest to become #1 industry player.*	*Help T-TC develop viable, marketable products.*
Financial:	*At least double my current salary + bonuses.*	*Increase in salary to afford new mortgage payments and twins' future college tuition.*
Social:	*Opportunity to enhance international relationships.*	*Mutual sharing of skills and knowledge with new colleagues.*
Physical:	*Urban, fast-paced.*	*Same.*

Ellee has validated that her initial goals appear to be the right ones.

Success tip 7-3:

FOCUS ON YOUR STRENGTHS

According to recent employment polls, only 20 percent of workers get to do what they think they do best every day. Often (but not always), doing what you do best is also what you like doing. Being happy and successful in your work means you have to focus on your strengths. So learn what they are:

- Find out what you learn quickly. Usually that builds on similar skills and knowledge that you already have.
- Identify what gives you the most satisfaction. (If you have a stack of work to do, which do you want to tackle first?)
- Think about the kinds of things your colleagues and managers ask you to do. This is a clue to what others consider your strengths.
- Check out skills-assessment tests online or in other career books.
- Ask others for honest feedback. As well as family, friends and co-workers you like, ask your adversaries.

How about your deficits? You'll need to work on those as well. It is your outstanding strengths, however, that will most define you as an E^3 performer.

3. Who else cares and why?

Your Career, Inc. has a set of stakeholders. First of all, your company has a stake. As you gain experience and develop resources on your path to the next right job and strategic career, you can help your organization achieve its strategic goals. Your manager and co-workers also stand to benefit.

Your stakeholders also include your family, close friends and mentors who, by their proximity and emotional ties to you, stand to gain or lose based on your decisions. They also have the power to advance or impede your career campaign.

Your past and present colleagues have a stake. If you land a great new job or start your own business, you may recruit them. If you move to a new industry in an elevated position, you increase their networks by virtue of your new associations. If you embark on volunteer work, you enrich that organization and increase its potential as well as improving the reputation of your company as one that is committed to giving back to the community.

➠ SNAPP™ it!

Consider the major stakeholders in your career and your next right career step. Fill in all the names that apply, and tell why these people are likely to care.

Table 7-e Who else cares and why?

	Names	Why do they care?
Immediate family		
Extended family		
Friends		
Network of professional associates outside the company		
Current manager		
Mentors (internal & external to company)		
Others in your company		
Others in your department		
Customers and vendors		
References		
Constituents of volunteer agencies		
Others		

 **Ellee considers her support team.**

Table 7-e Who else cares and why?

	Names	*Why do they care?*
Immediate family	*Children Dakota and Robin*	*Larger house, college education, role model for their future careers*
Extended family Network of professional associates outside the company	*Parents and sister, names in Rolodex®, PDA and contact system*	*Proud of me, increase their network*
Manager	*Frank*	*On the move himself; likes to support all employees in growth*
Mentors	*Gracie, Halim, Floyd*	*Want my growth and development and T-TC success*
Others in the department team	*Everyone on the team*	*Opens new opportunities for them when I move on*

4. What do I have to offer?

Career management is essentially a highly personalized marketing campaign for *Your Career, Inc.* Knowing your strengths will help you identify an occupational fit and then effectively package your product.

Potential employers will be interested in your knowledge, skills and experience in the functional area. They will want to know about your:

- Knowledge of the industry, the issues, the company, the division, the competition, the work itself and the world at large. Do you have success secrets that may not be well known?
- Experience in this field or industry. What variety of jobs have you held? How long? What resources can you employ? What is the strength of your network?
- Functional strengths and quantifiable abilities. Do you hold degrees and certifications? Can your accomplishments be objectively tested and measured? Examples are managing cash, developing computer systems, introducing new products, reorganizing work teams, increasing productivity and reducing overhead.

Employers are also interested in your enterprising E^3 nature. They will make judgments based on these attributes:

- **Entrepreneurial:** This is your ability to (a) package your capabilities into valuable products that meet identified needs, and (b) provide this significant value to your employer or clients. It is the extent to which you own your future and take responsibility for doing everything necessary and appropriate to fulfill your vision. It includes your knowledge of the competition, the strategic alliances you create and your ability to adapt your vision to evolving conditions.
- **Excellent:** This is your command of general business, your industry and your company. It includes the skills with which you perform your job. It includes other excellent people you enlist to help, your constant commitment to learning and gaining new skills, your credibility and the extent to which you share your expertise effectively with others.
- **Engaging:** This is your ability to work with people in a way that makes the team a success. It includes the extent to which you are easy to work with and indispensable to the team in order to get things done. Increasingly, employers are placing more weight on people skills.

When developing your career plan, consider how you are developing all three areas. Once you identify your knowledge, experience, skills and enterprising attributes, you will be able to identify your various options for packaging these strengths into your own value proposition – the overall "product" you will offer an employer or client.

➠ SNAPP™ it!

List the products employers would be willing to buy under each of the categories below.

Table 7-f What do I have to offer?

	Strengths
Knowledge	
Experience	
Functional strengths	
E^3 skills	

 **Ellee determines her strengths.**

Table 7-f What do I have to offer?

	Strengths
Knowledge	• *Deep understanding of the industry, company and marketing* • *Extensive industry network*
Experience	• *Sales, marketing, advertising*
Functional strengths	• *Project management – getting things done* • *Solid communications (speaking, writing)*
E^3 skills	• *Highly entrepreneurial and excellent*

5. What knowledge, skills and abilities will I need?

If you've set goals that will stretch you beyond your current abilities and comfort zone, you will need to expand your current set of skills and knowledge. This may mean further education, training or other targeted activities. At this point, you may not know enough about your strategic career or even your next right career step to complete a detailed plan. Remember that you are still in the visionary stage. You will build your action plan – which will include research and plans for implementation – in A = Act on It.

➠ SNAPP™ it!

Identify the steps you will need to take in these four areas:

Table 7-g What knowledge, skills and abilities will I need?

	Strategic career goal	Next right career step
Knowledge		
Experience		
Functional strengths		
E^3 skills		

 **Ellee identifies her development needs.**

Table 7-g What knowledge, skills and abilities will I need?

	Strategic career goal	*Next right career step*
Knowledge	*Thorough knowledge of global economy* *International relations*	*Product development* *Contacts in manufacturing*
Experience	*Product management*	*Global experience, management*
Functional strengths	*Management of complex budget*	*Enhance project management, strategic global products marketing*
E^3 skills	*Leadership skills*	*Increase listening and people management skills*

Success tip 7-4:

TURN EVERY JOB INTO A PROJECT

Keeping in mind that every job is potentially the "next right step" on the path to your ideal career, you'll increase your odds of success when you think of each new one as a project with a beginning, middle and end. Try to visualize the end of the project first. This becomes your guide to the steps you will take along the way.

Regardless of where you are in your current job, ask yourself these questions:

- What will it look like when I'm doing it right?
- What do I want to accomplish in this job?
- What do I want to learn?
- What skills do I want to acquire or hone?
- What new contacts will be important for future positions?
- When I have moved on, what will others say has been my contribution to this job, department, division, company and industry?

Ellee realizes that both her strategic career goal and next right career step will require additional education and training. Since she cannot afford to stop working while acquiring new skills, she begins to think about how to fit corporate training and on-the-job training into her busy schedule.

Based on her self-assessment of engaging attributes, Ellee recognizes a shortfall in her communications skills. Although she is good at speaking, recent 360° feedback indicates a need to improve her listening skills and increase the frequency and depth of the information she shares with others. Enhancing her entrepreneurial and excellence skills will also be helpful. Ellee thinks she can tackle these with no further formal training, but rather by crafting an action plan that will remind her to regularly review sound business practices and to increase the quality and quantity of her written and verbal communication. She thinks these enhanced skills will even improve her relationship with the children.

Document S = See It findings

Now that you have completed all the tables and answered all the questions, record your strategic career goal.

In 3 to 5 years, I will ______________________________

Now record your next best step.

Within 6-12 months, I will ___________________________

Post these goals where you can view them regularly.

Success tip 7-5:

DEVELOP A MENTOR

Mentors in the corporate world are individuals who help others progress along their chosen paths. Mentors can be managers, but not all managers are effective mentors.

Most people who have successfully risen in their organizations and professions have benefited from some level of mentoring. If you don't have a mentor, you can develop one.

Begin by identifying a potential mentor and then asking for an informational interview to answer your questions about the field and what it takes to succeed. Here's how.

- Identify people in your network who can provide introductions. Tell your contacts what you want to achieve and why, and ask for their assistance.
- Using the introduction, contact a potential mentor and invite him/her to coffee or lunch. Be clear about why you want this informational meeting.
- Prepare by developing a list of targeted questions. Among them, include some queries about his/her approach to success. There should be evidence of a conscious plan and process.
- At the meeting, do some ego-stroking. If the person is interested in your questions and receptive to them, you may have the makings of a mentor.
- Follow up with a hand-written thank you letter or e-mail.

Summary

At this point, you should have a general picture of the what, why and who of your strategic career and your next right career step. You also have a good idea about your current strengths and a general idea about what additional steps you'll need to take to qualify for all your planned moves, including work on the gaps in your E^3 profile.

Before leaving Chapter 7, review your notes and tables you have completed. Ask:

- Does my strategic career goal still look like something I'd like to do?
- Does my next right career step lead in the direction of my strategic career?
- Will my strategic career and my next right career step meet the needs and wants of my stakeholders and me?
- Given the gap between my current abilities and the E^3 attributes I'll need, am I willing to make that investment?

If the answer to all these questions is yes, then move on to N = Negotiate It. If one or more of the answers is no, revisit S = See It, and make adjustments to your goals before moving on.

You will validate your next right career step as you work through Chapter 8. For now, however, this provides an excellent starting point.

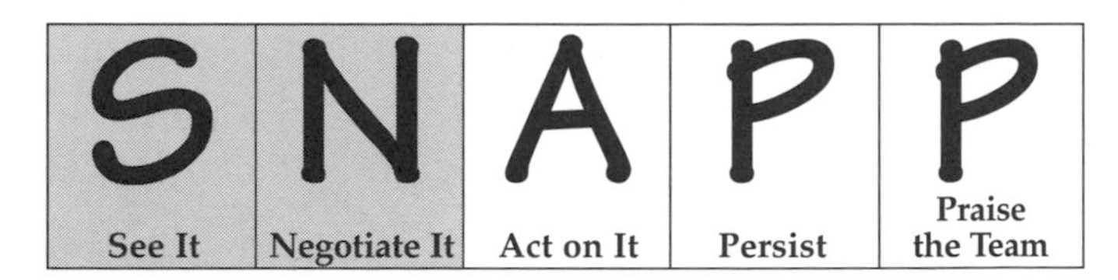

Chapter 8: N = Negotiate It

From here on, the focus shifts. You will continue to keep one eye on your strategic career, but your major effort will be to reach your next right career step.

In N = Negotiate It, you work out the details. (In SNAPP™ terminology, "negotiate" means navigating the maze to your next right step.) The questions are:

1. What is the scope of the effort?
2. What are the assumptions?
3. Who will help?
4. What can change or go wrong?
5. What are the financial implications?

1. What is the scope of the effort?

One of the big questions you must answer early on is how much effort you are willing to expend to achieve this career step. How many potential new departments or employers will you consider? What positions won't you consider? How much additional training or formal education are you willing to acquire? What time frame is acceptable?

Because first choices are not always available, it's wise to identify second choices. For example, if it's imperative that you change jobs and there are no jobs within your company that fit your criteria, you may have to look outside even though there may be some unwanted side effects such as lengthening your commute or relocating. Keep in mind, however, that in the revolving door of today's job marketplace, it may be possible to leave a company in good stead and then return after a period of time with no ill will – and often at an elevated position because of your new skills and abilities. True E^3 employees are a scarce commodity with generally many options.

➠ SNAPP™ it!

Complete the following matrix. The list is not all-inclusive; add other factors and make changes that are pertinent to you. You have already identified some of the factors in Table 7-a of S = See It. Be alert for any inconsistencies among answers in Tables 7-a and 8-a.

Identify first choices and in some cases viable alternatives. Then, make another pass, starring four or five of your highest priorities. These may become your non-negotiables.

Table 8-a Scope of efforts for the next right step:

Factors	First choice job	Second choice job
Inside my company		
What position (level, title) will I accept?		
Which departments will I consider?		
How much training will I need?		
How many people and at what levels will I contact?		
Where am I willing to relocate?		
Are there any physical or environmental issues?		
Outside my company		
What industries will I investigate?		
What size companies?		
Public or private?		
Type/level of work?		
Relocation?		
Compensation?		
Others?		

 **Ellee considers the scope of her search.**

Since Ellee works for a large company with a number of departments and positions that can serve her next step needs, she does not consider looking externally. She places stars next to her highest priority items.

Table 8-a Scope of efforts for the next right step:

Factors	First choice job	Second choice job
Inside my company		
Position (level, title)	*Product Manager, grade 10*	*Brand manager, grade 9*
Department	*Global*	*Domestic*
Hours/schedule	*No change**	*No change*
Training	*Paid, off-site*	*On-the-job*
Compensation	*Additional $10,000*	*No change*
Relocation	*No**	*Suburban office*

2. What are the assumptions?

When projects of any kind fail, it is often because assumptions were not clarified up front. People frequently assume that essential conditions exist when they don't, and conversely fail to see important aspects of reality that can get in the way. False assumptions that are not addressed can impede progress and result in career grief.

For example:

Early in her career, Ellee had heard that technical writing was a growing field with great demand and excellent salaries. She knew she was a good writer and liked figuring out new things. At substantial expense in terms of both tuition and time away from the family, Ellee enrolled in a two-year certification program offered in the evenings. She had done no research on what technical writing jobs really entailed, so she was unprepared for the sometimes isolated environment in which technical writers operate.

Ellee's first (and last) job as a technical writer ended only six months after she started. She found herself out of the mainstream and lacking in the extensive people contact she had assumed was part of any business environment. Despite her excellent technical writing skills and initial high motivation, Ellee never liked the work. Not only was her skill and experi-

Success tip 8-1:

DOUBLE CHECK ANSWERS

When making key career decisions, check more than one source. In interviews, it is only natural for corporate managers to put the company in the best light. They usually deliver the party line, when actual practice may be different.

For example, a leading professional services firm was an early adopter of the "flat organization." In some ways, the firm succeeded in its efforts to reduce or eliminate hierarchy; managers and directors not only tolerated but fully encouraged the dissent and constructive criticism of even the most junior team members. Through habit or necessity, however, the organization remained hierarchical in other ways. Associates joked, "I know this is a non-hierarchical organization; my boss told me so."

This type of mixed performance is not a failure, but rather a partial and still laudable success. Organizations, like people, are always full of good intentions. If they deliver only partly on their more lofty aspirations, that may be considered reasonable performance.

When interviewing for a position in a company with which you are not familiar, double check. Search the Web site for clues about what they offer. Tactfully ask several different employees "in the trenches" about the corporate culture and the way things really work.

There's no fool-proof way to know everything in advance. Gather information to the extent possible, and then go with your intuition.

ence in technical writing of little value in her ensuing job search, but it actually put off some potential employers who categorized her in a technical support role rather than marketing. "If I'd known all this before," Ellee said, "I would have used the time and money to further develop some other aspect of my career."

Even experienced career managers often view new positions through rosy lenses. They embark on a job or career change with preconceived ideas about the needs of the employer (customer), their own capabilities and how the new position will fill their needs and wants.

The most critical assumption career managers can make is that they have a set of viable and marketable skills that an employer (customer) is willing to buy. When preparing your career development plan, be sure to investigate and back up these assumptions. The following table lists some assumptions and the questions you may want to ask.

Assumptions about your qualifications

Assumption	Questions to validate
1. This department/ company needs my services.	What is the job description? What are the department's/company's current competency gaps?
2. This department/ company wants my services.	What unique product do I offer? What is the competition – human or technological, internal or external?
3. I have the skills, abilities and track record to fill the position.	Is my resume up to date, and does it apply to the job I'm seeking? Is my education adequate? Are all my Es covered?
4. The timing is right.	Is the company/department ready to make this change? Am I in the right position to make this move?

Other big assumptions center on whether the job you are seeking really will be your next right career step. Consider these questions along with others that pertain to the change you are seeking.

Assumptions about your qualifications

Assumption	*Questions to validate*
1. This job is what it promises and is a good career step for me.	*Does it fit my strategic career goal?*
2. This job will be interesting and challenging in its own right.	*I may be doing this job for several years. Is it what I want to do? What is the attitude of others in this department/company – engaged and productive or bored and angry?*
3. This department/ company will offer opportunities for growth.	*Is the business increasing? Is the product/ service "need to have" or "nice to have?" Is innovation encouraged? Is training available?*
4. I will be able to easily move on when I'm ready.	*What is the history and experience of others in this department/company with regard to advancement potential?*
5. This department/ company has a solid future.	*What is the perception of this department by others in the company – cutting edge or lackluster?*
6. The department/ company strategy and plans fit with my own.	*How well do the strategic goals and expectations of the prospective employer fit with my own goals and preferences? How would the value I provide fit those goals?*
7. The corporate culture will be a good fit with mine.	*How does the organization expect people to interact? Is it a flat organization or hierarchical, democratic or autocratic, structured or loosely managed? What kind of style and work habits does an employee need to build credibility in that particular organization? What kind of "corporate citizen" is this company?*

SNAPP™ it!

Using the previous lists as a model, identify at least ten assumptions about your career move. Then prepare questions you might ask yourself and others to validate the assumptions.

♣ **Ellee lists her assumptions about her next right career step: Product Manager for Global Products Division**

Examples:

- *There will be an open position at my level or above that matches my needs and wants.*
- *I can find people in the company and/or Global Products Division who will provide referrals for an open position.*
- *I have sufficient skills and abilities to qualify for the position.*
- *I can learn the job quickly enough to retain my reputation as a quick study and top performer.*

3. Who will help?

Every project has a team. As project manager of your career management campaign, you will identify and enlist supporters. Most will be network contacts with the power to advance your efforts. They generally fall into the following categories:

- **Company contacts** such as managers, senior executives and co-workers at all levels.
- **Mentors,** both internal and external, who have the requisite knowledge and resources and who are sincerely interested in helping. (E^3 employees generally have the easiest time attracting mentors.)
- **Industry experts** in your current profession and/or profession of choice. Arrange informational interviews with leaders of trade associations, professional societies, unions, professors and alumni. Include people in similar functions and at your same level in other organizations.
- **Career management experts** such as human resource professionals in your company, career counselors at your *alma mater*, personal coaches in private practice, self-help books, Web sites, recruiters and individuals in career networking groups. Many large companies offer professional coaching as a benefit. If your company does, take advantage of it.
- **Personal contacts** including friends and relatives, former colleagues from school and employment, volunteer activities and clubs, professors and professionals such as your doctor, dentist and accountant.

While you cannot count on anyone else to take charge of your career, be on the lookout for willing assistants.

Success tip 8-2:

PRACTICE CONTROL/NO CONTROL

There are some things you can change, and some things you cannot. Learning to differentiate the two saves time and mental stress. When it appears there are "no control" conditions, consider the aspects you can control. Then, make a plan for action.

Example #1:

No control: When applying for a new position, you generally cannot control the specific requirements of the job and the initial job role.

Control: You can determine whether the job fits your criteria for your "next right step" and your career strategy. Based on your assessment, you can control whether or not you accept the position.

Example #2:

No control: The job you most want may not be available when you're ready to move ahead.

Control: You can manage your career by always having two or three viable and desirable options. This increases the odds that you can take a next right step whenever you're ready. There's another advantage as well. Facing the option of losing you to another department or company, employers sometimes create positions for promising E^3 employees.

In the career game, your E^3 attributes are your most valuable assets. They provide the greatest "control" options when events otherwise might seem out of your control.

➠ SNAPP™ it!

If you manage your team effectively, the contacts you develop will serve you in this and subsequent campaigns.

List at least 25 people who could serve on your team. Use the categories listed above or develop your own. You will learn how to handle this list in P = Persist.

If you interview for new positions outside your company, you will need character and industry references. From your list of 25, identify four to five credible, positive and enthusiastic people who will vouch for your ability, expertise, successes, integrity and skills.

4. What can change or go wrong?

A word of caution. A change in job and career always entails unforeseen risks. No matter how thorough you are, there will nearly always be assumptions that you miss and that can potentially derail your efforts.

Examples

Here are some troublesome events that you have no way of predicting. The intent is not to frighten you, but to demonstrate that even the best crafted plans can come unglued:

- Your company is acquired. Duplication of jobs causes restructuring and layoffs. You are one of them.
- Management changes shortly after you accept the position. The new boss brings in a niece to do the job you were promised.
- A downturn in the economy or market forces drastic downsizing. The job changes significantly or is eliminated.
- The company is restructured, and your department or job no longer exists.
- You make some false assumptions about how well you will like the new position.

Some pitfalls can be avoided by considering them in advance. For example, your industry and company research may reveal trends that might change your goals and strategy.

In any case, your best contingency plan is the strategy you have already begun: becoming an enterprising employee and career manager at the top of your game. Top-notch professionals will always be in demand.

Remember, too, that not all change is bad. Sometimes advantageous events occur – even when events initially appear ominous. It is not uncommon for employees who experience a layoff to realize shortly thereafter that it was in fact a serendipitous event. Forced to re-examine their goals and priorities, they find new life in a new vocation.

➠ SNAPP™ it!

Re-examine your goals and assumptions. Then list the things that may change or go wrong. Your list of assumptions from the previous step is a good starting point, but don't stop there. For each possible change, consider an alternate action if the assumption proves false.

Table 8-b What can change or go wrong?

Assumption	Action if assumption proves false
1.	
2.	
3.	
4.	

♣ Ellee makes contingency plans.

Here are two in Ellee's list of ten things that can change or go wrong.

Table 8-b What can change or go wrong?

Assumption	*Action if assumption proves false*
1. This job is what it promises to be and is a good career step for me.	*I will train my assistant to take over so I can move on ASAP.*
2. This job will be interesting and challenging in its own right.	*I will use the opportunity to learn this part of the business - and plan never to work here again!*

5. What are the financial implications?

Financial considerations often play an important role in career management decisions. Changes in job and career can affect you positively or negatively. Here are some possible effects and suggestions for ways to handle them:

Consideration	How to handle
Downward changes in salary, compensation and benefits.	Negotiate for an increase or offsetting perks.
Need for increased education and training.	Ask your manager or HR representative about in-house training programs and tuition matching and reimbursement.
Wardrobe can be dress up or dress down.	Dress in tune with the formal and informal dress codes. Strive to dress up "one notch."
Commute fees can increase or decrease.	If significant increase, be ready to negotiate for consideration or flexible schedule.
Relocation.	If costs are not covered, be ready to negotiate.

➠ SNAPP™ it!

Consider the financial implications of a new job.

- What expenses will be associated with the change? Can you afford them?
- What possible gains will you realize? How can you best invest the proceeds?

Summary

You have now considered every angle of your next career move:

- **The scope:** The number of potential new departments, companies and industries you'll consider, whether you're willing to relocate, what level of position you will accept and compensation factors.
- **Your assumptions:** The "givens" you expect in a new position or career and the associated questions to validate them.
- **Who will help:** A list of at least 25 potential team members from inside and outside your company, mentors, industry experts, career managers and personal contacts.
- **What can change or go wrong:** The actions you'll take if your assumptions prove false or situations change.
- **The financial implications:** How you plan to handle the deficits and the surpluses associated with your proposed changes.

Take a few minutes to review your stated next right career step and all other notes to make sure you are committed to making the change. In the next chapter, you will build an action plan to take you to your next right career step.

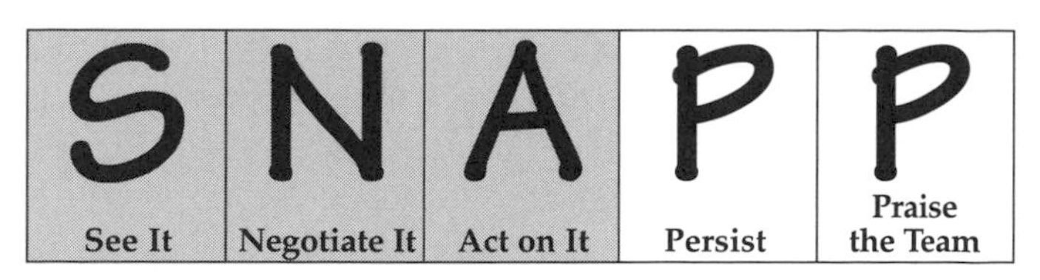

Chapter 9: A = Act on It

SNAPP™ shot

To succeed in your career, you must have a plan.

Once you have a clear vision of your next right career step and how it fits into your ideal career, you can lay out a tactical action plan, also known as a career development plan, and assign accountability. The three A = Act on It questions are:

1. What's the action plan?
2. Who is accountable?
3. Who will support it?

1. What's the action plan?

A project manager's most important tool is the action plan. It is critical in the planning stage and later in the follow-through. It serves as a constant reminder and tracking device until the project is complete. Afterward, it serves as documentation.

In the case of career management, you will have two types of plans which you will work and track simultaneously.

- The **master plan** lists all the tasks that lead you both to your ideal career and your next right career step.
- **Specific plans** cover targeted, tactical actions to enhance your E^3 abilities and secure your next right career step. You may have several of these at once.

The master plan

Every master plan will be somewhat different, depending on individual career goals, individual strengths and resources. The following outline can be your starting point.

The major tasks are in bold, followed by more detailed supporting steps. Although the tasks are numbered, they are not necessarily sequential. For example, "Develop and maintain your network" is numbered 6, but these key tasks rightly occur throughout the process – and throughout life.

The master plan also suggests the frequency for many of the actions. Note that these are guidelines, not absolutes. Determine your own frequency of occurrence based on your personal experience and interests.

Depending on the tickler system you use – electronic or paper-based – you can set reminders about when to take various actions. One system that you should not rely on, however, is your memory. Without a disciplined approach to career management, it is too easy to let other priorities take precedence. (Methodologies are covered in greater detail in Chapter 10, P = Persist.)

If you have been completing all of the SNAPP™ It! exercises to this point, you have already performed many of these tasks in the master plan.

Suggested Master Plan for Career Management

	Task	Each week	Each month	Each quarter	Each year	3-5 years
1.	**Perform an in-depth self-assessment.**					
1-a	Identify interests and skills				X	
1-b	Summarize areas of knowledge and functional expertise.				X	
1-c	List portable skills.				X	
1-d	Take online interest and skills assessments.					X
1-e	Write out professional accomplishments or war stories.			X		
1-f	Consider and rank 2 to 3 career options.				X	
2.	**Evaluate career options.**					
2-a	Identify industry or industries.				X	
2-b	Select level of position.				X	

Task	Each week	Each month	Each quarter	Each year	3-5 years
2-c Define type of work.				X	
2-d Develop core value requirements.					X
2-e Research job qualifications and requirements.				X	
2-f Identify any gaps between self-assessment and job requirements.				X	
2-g Identify steps to take to fill the "gaps" in relation to goals and the career development plan.			X		
3. Identify your ideal career goal and next right career step.					
3-a Decide on ideal career goal.					X
3-b Decide on next right career step.				X	
3-c Review and assess next right career step.			X		
4. Develop marketing materials.					
4-a Create biographical materials including accomplishments, awards and war stories.				X	
4-b Review biographical materials.				X	
4-c Update resume and bio.			X		
4-d Develop a summary statement and "elevator pitch."				X	
5. Monitor the industry.					
5-a Read industry news.		X			
5-b Attend professional association meetings.		X			
5-c Review the want ads and visit job Web sites.			X		

	Task	Each week	Each month	Each quarter	Each year	3-5 years
5-d	Keep current with global and industry news.		X			
5-e	Identify trends.			X		
6.	**Develop and maintain your network.**					
6-a	Prepare/update contacts lists.			X		
6-b	Develop lists of companies.				X	
6-c	Conduct informational interviews.			X		
6-d	Develop/consult a mentor.		X			
6-e	Develop and maintain a communications plan.					X
6-f	Thank the team.		X			
6-g	Celebrate victory.		X			
7.	**Monitor your performance.**					
7-a	Check progress against work targets.		X			
7-b	Review work priorities to ensure you're on target.		X			
7-c	Volunteer outside work group.			X		
7-d	Continue your education.				X	
7-e	Participate in professional societies or charitable organizations.				X	
7-f	Confer with your mentor.				X	
7-g	Enhance personal marketing materials.				X	
7-h	Obtain manager's feedback.				X	
8.	**Develop Entrepreneurial skills.**					
8-a	Write articles.			X		

Task	Each week	Each month	Each quarter	Each year	3-5 years
8-b Give speeches.			X		
8-c Deliver workshops.			X		
8-d					
8-e					
9. Develop Excellence skills.					
9-a Develop team skills.			X		
9-b Increase job skills.			X		
9-c Coach/mentor others.		X			
9-d					
9-e					
10. Develop Engaging skills.					
10-a Make manager look good.	X				
10-b Be enthusiastic.	X				
10-c Listen to others.	X				
10-d Give credit to the team.	X				
10-e Celebrate individual and team accomplishments.	X				
10-f					
10-g					

➠ SNAPP™ it!

Develop a master plan of your own based on the one above. Add, change and delete items to make the plan applicable to your career goals. Maintain a copy that is easily accessible so you can review it frequently.

Success tip 9-1:

TAKE SMALL BITES

If you're faced with eating an elephant, the saying goes, start with small bites.

The prospect of developing plans to reach your next right career step may seem daunting. To calm your fears, restrict your efforts to one or two mini projects at a time. Breaking large tasks into manageable units will allow you to accomplish things every day or every week. Checking items off your list will demonstrate that you're making progress and give you a psychological boost that will help you persist.

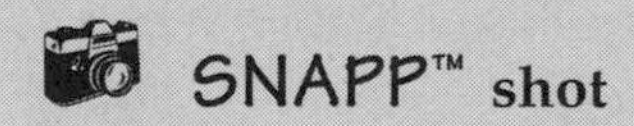

Capitalize on your strengths.

Specific plan

The master plan lists suggested actions under each of the E[3] tasks. You gathered information in the self-assessments in Chapters 2, 3 and 4. Now you will develop action plans to manage career projects in the near term. You may have several underway at once, all supporting your strategic career plan.

In developing specific action plans, remember to continue developing your unique strengths. These are what set you apart from the masses and make you marketable.

Your specific plans of action are more than to-do lists. They include names of resources and proposed start and end dates associated with each task. Complete the plan in enough detail that you leave nothing to chance. To establish dates, first determine your target for completion; then work backward through the plan. In general, the more specific the steps, the more useful the action plan will be to you in accomplishing your goals. You can use spreadsheet or word processing software, or simply pencil and paper.

♣ Ellee develops a specific action plan.

Ellee realizes that she should begin using her public speaking talents as a way of marketing herself professionally. Selection as a speaker at a global marketing conference will offer tremendous exposure. Since she has not yet presented at a conference, she knows that she will have to start small. She sets her sights on securing a spot on the program of the regional convention of marketing professionals. This convention usually takes place in November. It is now January, but Ellee knows that speakers are chosen months in advance, so it is not too early to begin the application process.

There generally are many speakers wanting to present, so even being selected for a local conference will involve more than a few quick phone calls. As Ellee begins to SNAPP™ this effort, she decides that co-presenting with a better-known speaker is probably her best opportunity. Selecting someone outside her company, T-TC, and forming a "joint venture" of sorts will offer advantages to her and the co-presenter.

If a speaking part is not possible under any circumstances, Ellee's contingency plan is to deliver one of the continuing education workshops. She is fairly confident that she can do this; one of the members of the education committee is a long-time associate who has frequently urged Ellee to deliver a workshop on "how to work a room." If this happens, her path to her ultimate goal of speaking at a global marketing convention may be delayed by a year or two, but Ellee is confident that if she persists, she will ultimately succeed.

Ellee completes the S and N of SNAPP™ for this project, outlining how she "sees" it (a spot on the list of general session speakers); why she wants to do this (exposure for herself and T-TC and increased networking possibilities); her "customers" (conference attendees and T-TC); her resources (professional network, fellow presenter, T-TC legal reviewer), assumptions (her position at T-TC is sufficiently senior), her budget (she plans that T-TC will pay her expenses if she is selected); and what can change or go wrong (i.e., she will not be accepted this year, her company will not release her to participate or will refuse to pay her way).

Ellee's specific action plan appears as follows:

Action plan for presenting at regional conference

Task	Name of Resource	Start Date	Due Date	Comments
1. Apply to present	**Ellee**			
1-a Call conference secretary for dates and application form.	"	1/8	1/10	
1-b Complete forms.	"	1/15	2/18	
1-c Submit forms to conference.	"	2/28	2/28	
2. Network for information & to find co-presenter	"			
2-a Contact network to learn ins and outs of being selected.	"	1/8	1/15	
2-b Contact mentor for names of references and co-presenter.	"	1/8	1/10	
2-c Contact references and ask permission.	"	1/15	2/14	
2-d Contact potential co-presenters.	"	1/15	1/30	
3 Prepare topic	**Ellee & co-presenter**			
3-a Research likely topics.	"	1/30	2/7	

Task	Name of Resource	Start Date	Due Date	Comments
3-b Develop presentation outline.	"	*2/7*	*2/15*	
3-c Finalize outline.	"	*2/15*	*2/18*	
4. Obtain T-TC permission.	***Ellee***			
4-a Ask manager how to obtain T-TC permission.	"	*1/8*	*1/8*	
4-b Submit forms & topic to T-TC reviewers for authorization.	"	*2/18*	*2/18*	
4-c T-TC reviews and authorizes.	*Legal Dept.*	*2/18*	*2/27*	

Ellee develops two similar, separate action plans for publishing articles in a marketing trade journal and for improving her management communications skills.

➡ SNAPP™ it!

Prepare action plans to address your development needs.

- Revisit your "E" assessments in Chapters 2, 3 and 4.
- Identify several specific areas for improvement as well as enhancement and growth.
- Create a specific action plan for each one, using whatever software or paper-based system works for you. Ellee's matrix may serve as your model. These should be subsets of your master plan.
- Keep your action plans where you can access them readily and continually monitor your progress.

Success tip 9-2:

KEEP YOUR RESUME UP TO DATE

Your resume is your primary personal marketing tool. Maintain it as a text document on your computer in order to:

- ➤ Remind yourself of your strengths and experiences so you can continue to build on them.
- ➤ Remind yourself of things to talk about when there's an occasion to promote your skills, abilities and experiences.
- ➤ Provide you with an edge when a career opportunity suddenly arises and calls for a prompt response.

To keep your resume current, review it at least once a year, but quarterly is optimal. Several weeks prior to your annual performance evaluation, do this:

- ➤ Reflect on your many accomplishments for the year.
- ➤ Update your resume by listing the most impressive contributions you have made to your department and company. Be sure to include measurable results.
- ➤ Don't wait until your manager schedules a performance review. (In some departments or organizations this never happens.) Initiate the meeting yourself. Talk with your manager about your accomplishments, ask his/her advice about growth areas and enlist support for your initiatives. If your manager is unresponsive or unsupportive, this may be a clue that it's time to make plans to move on.

Also update your resume every time something significant occurs in your career: adding new responsibilities, changing jobs, receiving recognition, passing a significant milestone. Don't wait until the end of the performance year or cycle to update your resume and risk forgetting.

2. Who is accountable?

"Only YOU can prevent forest fires."

—Smokey the Bear

When project managers develop their action plans, they assign names to the owners of every task. As project manager of your own career, you will find it is your name that will appear most often in the resources column! (See Ellee's action plan on pages 106-107.) To the question "Who is accountable?" there can be only one answer. It is you, the owner and operator of *Your Career, Inc.*

3. Who will support it?

Enlisting others in support of your goals will be one of your greatest challenges and will test all your E^3 characteristics – most notably your engaging abilities.

Supporters likely will include the management of your company (generally, the higher in the organization they are, the greater their influence), mentors and individuals in your professional network. Do not overlook the importance of moral support from friends and family members who can both cheer you on and help pick you up when events don't go as planned.

SNAPP™ it!

Review the list of resources you prepared in N = Negotiate It (Who will help?). Tell these people about the goals you have set and if appropriate, show them your action plans. Ask for their moral support as well as their professional counsel.

♣ Ellee asks for support.

Ellee starts with her boss. She tells Frank about both her long-term and near-term career plans and asks for his support. Frank suggests a few minor changes to the plans and commits to assist. In addition, Ellee tells him about her plans to market herself by volunteering to speak at conferences and writing trade journal articles. She points out the advantage to T-TC of this kind of exposure, and he agrees. Frank promises to think about who inside or outside the organization can advise her.

Success tip 9-3:

DEVELOP A RESUME FOR YOUR STRATEGIC CAREER

Your strategic career goal is your vision of what you want your work life to be in three to five years. Although that may seem distant, you can begin to prepare by thinking in terms of the skills, experiences and education you'll need at the time.

Try these tactics:

- Imagine that you have an interview for the job you most want in three to five years.
- Prepare a job description for that work. What are likely areas and scope of responsibility? To what standards will you be held?
- Using your current resume as a starting point, develop a "strategic resume" adding the kinds of skills, work experiences and education you think would persuade the "customer" (your prospective employer) to buy your services.
- Keep this strategic resume where you can review it periodically.
- Turn the needed skills and abilities into projects with goals and action plans. Then set about making the resume a reality.

Summary

A = Act on It completes the planning stage of SNAPP™. You now have determined what it is that you want, negotiated the details of how to reach it and developed step-by-step action plans.

Keep your documentation of the S-N-A steps in a convenient place where you can find it and review it often. Maintain it in pencil or other easily updateable format. Remember that although your plans are now "set," you will continue to revisit and adjust them in the pursuit of your goals.

Here are some final tips on the planning stage of SNAPP™ from career management experts:

- Break down each major goal into a number of actionable and measurable objectives. Spread the objectives out over a reasonable time frame for you. For example, if a goal is to be met within a year, you don't have to do everything in the first week or month. Divide individual tasks over four quarters.
- Commit your objectives to specific action plans with "bite-sized" tasks, dates and assigned accountabilities.
- Enlist the help of people who know and support your goals and who will hold you accountable for meeting them. Plan to meet your supporters on a regular basis to give them updates and ask for suggestions.
- Plan to celebrate achievements along the way.

Success tip 9-4:

CONSIDER EXPERT CAREER COACHING

Chances are you don't cut our own hair, perform your own dentistry or personally draw up your own legal documents. For something as critical as your future, you may want to consider obtaining the counsel of a professional career coach.

What can a career coach do for you?

Career coaches are trained and devoted to increasing people's competence, commitment and confidence. They help individuals manage and facilitate effective career change and management. Through a variety of techniques and tools, they can help you:

- Objectively assess your strengths and developmental needs
- Gain awareness and focus to achieve agreed-upon goals
- Create a plan with results that are attainable, measurable and specific
- Identify and access different resources for learning and growing
- Celebrate successes and victories along the way.

How do you find the right one?

If your company offers career coaching, take advantage of it. If you are seeking a coach on your own, consider the following criteria. Expert career coaches should:

- Have previous experience coaching individuals
- Have experience in career assessment
- Know and understand a variety of corporate environments
- Understand career development and have effective techniques
- Be able to establish trust and intimacy with clients, respect confidentiality and be confrontational in a supportive way.

Many career coaches are independent consultants. You can find them through professional coaching societies such as the International Association of Career Management Professionals. Be sure to interview more than one, and ask for references from people in your network.

Personalities and styles of coaching differ. As you would with any practitioner, if you don't feel comfortable with and confident of the expertise of any coach, close the transaction and try another.

Chapter 10: P = Persist

 SNAPP™ shot

Little by little does the trick.

—Aesop, 6th century, B.C.

Planning a project is creative and fun. You get to imagine how things will be when you reach your career destination. You get to plot the course and share your vision with ardent supporters.

Now comes the truly hard part: implementation. Because you are already employed and must expend significant time and energy in the performance of the job that pays your rent, the temptation will be to relegate your career plans to the back burner. It is even more difficult to stay focused and motivated on the next career move when you're still excited about your current job or when things go wrong with your career plan.

The three steps in the planning stage of SNAPP™ are sequential, each one building on its predecessors. In the implementation stage, however, you perform the two steps concurrently. They are:

P = Persist

P = Praise the Team

In the P = Persist step, you will continually revisit and accomplish key tasks on your action plans – at least two lists at a time. P = Praise the Team is your regular celebration of the support you receive from others.

The action plan you developed in A = Act on It will guide your efforts every day. You cannot go further in SNAPP™ without it.

Success tip 10-1:

PERFORM REGULAR CHECK-UPS

Essential to every E^3 career manager is periodic performance assessment. In addition to the kind your manager provides annually or semi-annually, you need to perform self-assessments monthly or quarterly to make sure your efforts are still on track. Why? Because it's easy to get involved in your everyday job and forget to think strategically about your career. Put your check-ups on the calendar or in your contact system, and then follow through. Here's a possible schedule.

If you're new in a role, perform this check-up **monthly**. Ask:

- In the past month, I worked on A, B, C. Was I on target with respect to my job? With respect to my career goals?
- In the upcoming month, are my priorities the same? Why or why not?

Everyone should ask these questions at least **quarterly**:

- What have I done to continue my education?
- What have I volunteered to do (committee or task force) that is beyond the scope of my job description?
- Have I participated in a professional society or charitable organization?
- What kind of feedback have I received from my manager? (If the answer is "nothing," initiate a mini-review with your boss about a current project or goal.)
- Have I located or talked with a prospective internal mentor?
- Have I located or talked with a prospective external mentor?
- Have I reviewed and enhanced my personal marketing materials?

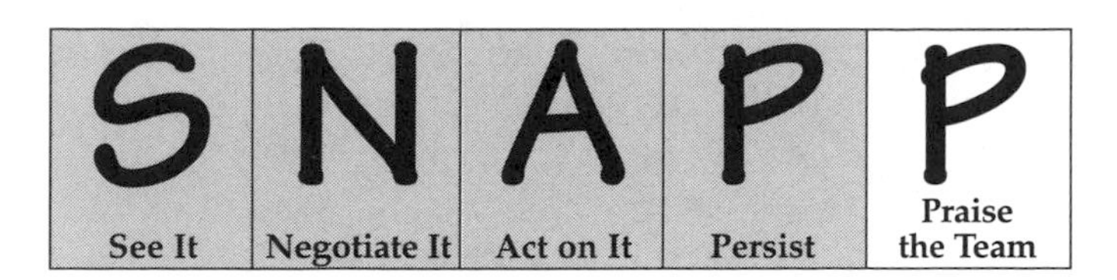

P = Persist

Success in working your action plans will require your positive energy, attention and stamina. It also will require significant know-how. You will have to create and communicate your own sense of urgency. You will have to manage a team of supporters, and often be your own coach, cheerleader and scorekeeper all at the same time. The payoff will come when you execute the plans well and get the promotion or secure the next right career step because of your efforts.

The P = Persist steps are:

1. Mind the details and keep score.
2. Recruit and retain your team.
3. Develop and maintain a communications package.
4. Stay focused.
5. Play the role of the position you seek.

1. Mind the details and keep score.

 SNAPP™ shot

If it is not tracked, it will not be done.

No matter how excellent your action plans and your intentions, if you don't pay attention to the details and keep track of results, you will not be successful.

Mind the details

As you work through each task, give the same attention to detail as you do to your current job. Just as you make time for your important clients and commitments, make time for your network and the deadlines on your career action plans. For example, prepare for an informational interview with a prospective mentor just as you would for a presentation to senior management. Determine your goal for the outcome of the interview, review the S-N-A document and plan your questions in advance. Following the meeting, record your notes and file them. Send a thank-you. This kind of attention to detail will demonstrate to your potential mentor that you're worth the investment of time and energy.

The groundwork you lay today is key to achieving your next right career step and ideal career goal.

Keep score

Set a schedule for reviewing your action plans using whatever technique works best for you. Whether you decide on a paper-based organizer, computer program/spreadsheet, personal data assistant (PDA) device or even a monthly calendar that you check off regularly, the format should be convenient.

Then, when you encounter the reminder, you will have to muster the discipline to act on it within a reasonable amount of time. For example, when it's Monday morning and you open your organizer or contact system to find that it's time to take a career management step, pledge to yourself that you'll attend to it within the day. If you have made the step small enough, you should be able to find time for it.

Use your tracking system to mark items off the list to demonstrate progress toward your goal. This will provide a sense of accomplishment and help keep you motivated.

➡ SNAPP™ it!

Develop a system of tracking that works for you. Develop quality standards for your own performance, promising yourself what you will accomplish within your own set timeframe. Make a plan for periodically reviewing your list. Check things off to show progress.

♣ Ellee prepares to keep score.

Upon completing her master action plan, Ellee programs reminders for an entire year using the reminder feature of her desktop computer contact system. To her surprise, the task takes less than 30 minutes. She sets them all to pop onto the computer monitor when she first logs on in the morning. That allows her to schedule the career to-dos into her day. She promises herself that she'll always try to complete the tasks before day's end. If she must push a task to the next day, she decides, she'll handle it before anything else.

2. Recruit and retain your team.

SNAPP™ shot

The people in your personal network are part of your career management team.

Effective project managers understand the value of the team. They are constantly recruiting members for current and potential projects, and for both professional and personal aspirations. Once enlisted, team members require special handling.

Recruiting your team

"Networking" is the common method for informally recruiting a team. It is the process of sharing information and support in both professional and personal settings. It is a reciprocal process that is understood by all parties who willingly provide ideas, leads and suggestions in exchange for ideas, leads and suggestions.

E^3 career managers spend a significant amount of time actively networking. Although people engaged in networking activities often appear to be just having a good time – going to lunch, chatting with friends about personal subjects, participating in recreation and sports – valuable relationships are being built that can be traded for goods, services and opportunities at a later date.

When recruiting individuals to your professional network, look for people who possess skills, knowledge and abilities in areas that complement your strengths. Be sure to include peers in other organizations, people who are doing the same things you are and fighting the same battles. The best recruits are other E^3 employees and career managers who have their own large networks that you can tap into by virtue of being acquainted.

Networking is a powerful way to expand your career options at any time – not just when you're in the job market. It works as well for other aspects of your life – such as when you need the name of a landscaper, a referral to a dentist, or even a recommendation for the best place in the neighborhood to make photocopies.

Retaining your team

Handled skillfully, your network of team members is invaluable. In most cases, it is the key to your next right career step.

Success tip 10-2:

DEVELOP YOUR NETWORK

Networking is the single most important ongoing task of any career manager. Here are some *how-tos* for developing your network.

➤ **Identify a base list of professional contacts.** Classify them by industry and job function. Begin with people you know from your current and previous employment, as well as customers, suppliers and external consultants. This list is the first level of networking, which is not as productive as most people think. As you talk with these people, gather information about industries, companies and management as well as names and phone numbers of more people to contact. These will be your second, third and fourth level contacts, which generally are more useful.

➤ **Identify a base list of personal contacts.** List family, extended family, friends, relatives of friends, neighbors, people you know from special interest groups, religious group contacts, former classmates and professionals like your doctor, dentist and accountant.

➤ **Attend professional association meetings.** If you are not already part of a professional association, now is the time to join your local chapter, or at least attend the monthly meetings.

➤ **Volunteer for committees and task forces.** Participate in charity and alumni organizations.

➤ **Learn from the pros.** Identify people for your network who are excellent at networking. Add them to your network and learn from them. What events do they attend? Whom do they know? How do they handle themselves? How do they support others? Consider working with a professional coach to support you in your networking skill development or find a mentor.

Remember that effective networking is a reciprocal process. It is more than just knowing people. Networkers actively help one another to the mutual benefit of each. Frequent give and take will strengthen your network and keep it running smoothly.

Look for ways to stay in touch and build up credit in your networking bank so there will be a large deposit of good will when you're ready to make a withdrawal. Both sides should win in every contact. Practice the following tips as they apply to your network:

- Keep a running database of contact information, dates and any information you've collected.
- Send your contacts email with pertinent industry news, articles from trade journals and any other appropriate items.
- Flag important dates such as birthdays and company anniversaries.
- Always send congratulations for promotions, new jobs and project accomplishments.

A network of supportive team members is not something you develop in two days or two weeks or even two years. It evolves over a career and a lifetime, leading to solid business and personal relationships that can bring joy and satisfaction in themselves. You'll know you're becoming a successful networker when other E^3 individuals actively recruit and work to retain you.

SNAPP™ shot

Effective networkers follow the "Golden Rule." They give as much as they get.

Success tip 10-3:

KEEP UP THE CONTACTS

Periodic contact with network members is essential. You cannot call only when you need help. The larger your network, the more structured you will need to be in maintaining it. Here are some guidelines:

- Be sensitive to peoples' communication styles and desires. E-mail is relatively unobtrusive, but keep messages short.
- Frequency of communication varies by individuals, but be sure that you keep in touch even when you don't need assistance.
- A contact can be a phone call, e-mail or get-together. If it's easier, "batch" the contacts, handling them all in one session or on one day. If a quick touch is all that's called for, sending e-mail is sometimes the most expedient. It eliminates a lengthy conversation and the possibility that either of you will feel obligated to do more. You can compose the same e-mail message and copy it repeatedly. (Tip: Don't send a group e-mail if you want it to look like a personal touch.)
- What do you say when you initiate a "touch?" Just keep people updated on such things as what's currently happening (high level) in the industry, mutual associates or your projects and initiatives. If you're actively seeking a new position, let them know your goals and target dates. Ask for information, but never a job.
- As you network, you'll keep adding to your list of contacts. For a variety of reasons, you'll be dropping others. Strive to keep a core of at least 50 people in your career network at all times.

➠ SNAPP™ it!

Follow these guidelines for establishing and maintaining your all-important career network.

- **Recruiting:** Develop your own plan for recruiting team members on an ongoing basis. Strive to add 10 qualified new contacts per quarter. That's less than one per week.
- **Retaining:** Develop a plan to periodically keep in touch with 25 of your most valuable contacts. Quarterly is about right for most contacts unless you have a specific reason. Sound daunting? Do the math. It amounts to only two calls a week.

♣ Ellee tackles networking.

Ellee views everyone in her network as a friend. To track and maintain her friendships, she keeps her professional network names under a separate folder in her desktop system. She has the system programmed to remind her weekly of three names. On Monday evenings after the children are asleep, Ellee sits down to her computer and composes a short, topical business-related message. She copies the generic message one at a time into e-mail, personalizes it for each contact, and sends it. The entire process usually takes about 15 minutes.

Throughout the week it's common for her to receive four or five e-mail messages and sometimes a call or two from people in the network. Ellee is careful to update changes in address and business information in her contact file.

For more personal contact, Ellee tries to arrange a monthly luncheon with a revolving group of old and new contacts. Sometimes she arranges dates with two or three contacts at a time.

Success tip 10-4:

TAKE A STRATEGIC APPROACH TO COMMUNICATIONS

Establish yourself as an effective communicator. Before delivering any communication, whether written or oral, formal or informal, always know:

- **The audience** and its characteristics. Consider level in the organization, goals, tolerance for detail, and professional and personal styles (i.e., "big sky thinkers" or micro managers).
- **Your objective,** stated as a desired outcome, not a topic. For example, don't say, "Discuss the characteristics of ______ services." Do say, "Gain approval for _____ services."
- **Length.** Available time in person and available space in print are factors. Practice brevity. Delight your audience by delivering higher quality in less time and less space than they expected.
- **The message and support.** Always create at least a quick outline of your overall message and the three to five key points that best support it. Brief statements, rather than phrases, will help you organize your list into a persuasive story.
- **Your opening and closing.** Whether the communication is written or oral, start and end strongly. Begin with a story or a quick review that raises or implies the main question to be answered. Summarize your main message up front unless it is extremely controversial. Preview the main supporting points. End with a restatement of your key conclusions and recommendations.
- **The design of the communication.** If the audience has a favorite format, follow it unless there's a good reason to change. Make sure the format is practical and that it fits the function.
- **What you need to listen and look for.** The best communicators are good listeners. Allow time for questions and comments. When taking questions during a presentation, be sure to repeat the question before responding so everyone can hear.

3. Develop and maintain a communications package.

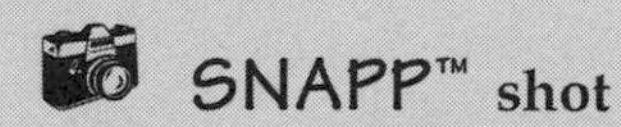

Effective communication is too important to leave to chance.

Lack of effective communications is one of the biggest stumbling blocks of any project. In terms of career management, there are at least three areas of communication that demand attention:

- Your team
- Potential purchasers of your services (employers)
- Prospective joint ventures and alliance partners.

As an enterprising E^3 employee and career manager, you will need effective marking materials – a "communications package" – to help you explain and promote yourself to all three.

Communications with your team

In order to help you achieve your goals, team members need to know where you're headed. Keep them updated on your strategy, challenges and accomplishments. As well as telling them about yourself, share appropriate project, industry and company news. The better informed supporters are, the better position they're in to assist you. It bears repeating that your communication plan is just an extension of your networking effort.

Communications with potential purchasers of your services

Effective networking is the single most important factor in the advancement of most people's careers. Even when you interview for prospective opportunities with people you know, you must be able to professionally market yourself both orally and in print. A professional quality presentation is even more important when your prospects are unknown to you.

With advance preparation and a current communications package, you'll be prepared to go "on stage" whenever you need to promote your services to potential employers and other purchasers of your services. Suggestions for the components of your communications package follow.

Success tip 10-5:

ALWAYS GO PREPARED

When the right things happen, it's seldom accidental. Enterprising career managers are always planning ahead. They leave nothing to chance.

Prior to every career contact or encounter, devote some time to preparation. The more important the event, the more time you should spend researching, considering all the angles and rehearsing.

Here's how the best salespeople prepare. Their actions can be summed up by the "4 R's:"

- **Remember** your goals for the encounter, and know exactly how this contact fits into your big picture.
- **Research** the industry, the organization and the person before the meeting. Prepare questions that will both add to your knowledge base and demonstrate you've done your homework.
- **Rehearse** your positioning statement (see page 126). Tailor it to the company and the situation. Prior to interviews, review the questions that typically arise; practice your answers.
- Be **Ready to close**. Know your desired next step, and be prepared to suggest it.

Communication with prospective joint ventures and alliance partners

As a professional in charge of *Your Career, Inc.*, you'll always be on the lookout for ways to leverage your own resources through alliances and joint ventures (see Success tip 2-1). Your marketing materials will be similar to the ones required for potential purchasers of your services. All begin with your vision of your strategic career and your carefully planned project approach.

Your communications package

Throughout your career, you'll be marketing yourself continuously. You'll be telling others about your goals, positions you want and why, and what value you'll add to the enterprise. To be prepared, you will need a full range of targeted materials that can be delivered in print and/or orally. Your communications package should include:

- **Resume:** This is a concise, usually bulleted list of your accomplishments and history of employment. It includes a positioning statement (see next page), a list of your positions held (including an accompanying brief description of the scope of responsibility and authority for each position), accomplishments, credentials and awards. Generally, resumes are geared to a specific job for which you are applying.
- **Bio:** This is generally a one-page summary of your work experience, education, special knowledge, skills and areas of expertise. It can include community involvement and brief personal information. The format is narrative in style. You will use a bio when asked to supply background information for your speaking engagements and to accompany articles you submit for publication. (See pages iii and iv of this book for examples of authors' bios.)
- **Endorsements:** These are letters, testimonials and other accolades that you have received for outstanding service. Ask the individuals who generated them if you may reproduce them. Maintain them in a file for use in brochures and other personal marketing materials.
- **Elevator pitch:** This is a short introduction (approximately 30 seconds) that describes who you are and other information such as the work you do. The purpose is to prepare the ground for meaningful conversation with people you have not previously met. It is called an "elevator pitch" because of its length; you should be able to deliver it succinctly to another person as you pass between floors in an elevator.

As part of your communications package, you will want to include the following components. Examples are from Ellee.

- A **positioning statement** is one succinct sentence or phrase that describes your function. You can use it in your resume, bio and cover letters and as your elevator pitch.

  Marketing professional for the Domestic Products Division of Tele-tele Corporation, competent in business analysis, market analysis and segmentation, relationship management and project management.

- A **summary** is a 50- to 75-word description of the value you have to offer. You can use this in a resume or bio.

  Innovative, entrepreneurial, analytic marketing manager with a proven track record of achieving goals, building brand value and maintaining top-line revenue and profit. Significant experience efficiently managing multi-million dollar budgets and effectively incorporating new technology and e-commerce applications into marketing, sales and customer service strategies. Strong analytical and problem solving skills. Believe in management by fact and data, but also comfortable with use of intuition in ambiguous situations. Strong communication skills and belief in individual and team accountability.

- **"War stories"** are accomplishment statements that back up your claims of experience and such skills and abilities as leadership, problem-solving and outstanding results. They provide real-life examples of the measurable value you've added to the business. They set the stage for further questions. You needn't write these down, but you should have two to three ready to relate.

  In early 2000, I began to independently research the need for a product with a set of features for building transaction-based mobile applications. When it appeared there might be a significant potential, I enlisted the support of colleagues from three different T-TC units. Together, we developed a proposal and accompanying action plan. We presented it to my division manager who located a senior management sponsor. I was made project manager of the cross-functional team that performed additional research, provided design input into the development effort and developed a workable and cost-effective marketing program. The project was completed on time and under budget. As a result of this project and successful product, the Domestic Products Division of T-TC exceeded its revenue targets by 30% and established itself as a leader in this technology.

You'll know you have an effective communications package when you can confidently deliver your elevator pitch on the spur of the moment and when you can update and deliver a bio or resume within an hour of a request.

⇒ SNAPP™ it!

Develop your own communications package.

- Review and revise your resume, updating it with your latest accomplishments and information.
- If you have a bio, review and revise it. If you don't have a bio, develop one now.
- Compose your positioning statement, a 50- to 75-word summary and several war stories.
- Practice delivering your 30-second elevator pitch, based on your positioning statement. Ask a trusted colleague to listen to your pitch and provide feedback. Revise if necessary.
- Think like a prospective employer as you review and revise your communications package. Ask: Why should this prospective employer buy my services? The answer should be evident in your materials and presentation.
- Devise a system for periodically reviewing and keeping all your materials current.

4. Stay focused.

SNAPP™ shot

Without focus, goals get fuzzy and then vanish.

Stay focused on your goals by devoting time each week to career management. Periodically review the S-N-A you documented in Chapters 7, 8 and 9. Don't be surprised, however, when conditions alter and the path you carefully plotted takes a different turn. Changes in the economy, your company's or department's leadership or your own interests can enter the picture with positive or negative consequences.

A positive change can provide the perfect job opportunity long before you expect it. When that happens, embrace the new opportunity, incorporate the new facts into your career plan and form a new plan earlier than you expected. That is serendipity.

Success tip 10-6:

STRIVE FOR BALANCE IN LIFE

Job satisfaction and career success are linked to a balanced and generally happy life. Here are some suggestions for enhancing your career – and life:

- **Confidence and optimism.** Love and accept yourself. Make a list of your accomplishments and congratulate yourself.
- **Forgiveness.** Forgive yourself for your mistakes. Analyze them and learn from them. Make changes and move on.
- **Economics.** Excessive worry about finances can cause you to take shortsighted and inappropriate actions. Minimize concerns by developing a budget and sticking to it. Adjust your standard of living so you can save money each month in order to provide a financial cushion and invest for the future.
- **Personal relationships.** Respect others. Develop a close, caring relationship with at least one other person and enjoy the company without expectations or demands.
- **Spirituality.** Enjoy nature, meditate, listen to music, think about your values.
- **Leisure.** Leave time in your day for enjoyable activities. Take weekends off.
- **Work.** Strive to be an enterprising employee and career manager. Explore options and be willing to change.
- **General.** Live a balanced life by getting into a variety of activities. Not only will this help you enjoy life, but it will also help you smooth over the career transitions and other rough spots you'll encounter.

When a not-so-welcome change occurs, try not to let it throw you off course. It may represent only a small setback. Regardless of the cause or severity, the remedy is always the same: Take a timeout, revisit the S-N-A, and test the vision, statements and assumptions. Adjust the parts that no longer appear true. Make sure that the remaining pieces still fit together. Begin again. Often, people find that what initially appeared to be a set-back turns out for the best.

➠ SNAPP™ it!

Allow time in your schedule for review and reflection at least once a quarter. Put it on your calendar. Then take 30 minutes to review and reflect on the things you documented in the S-N-A of SNAPP™.

- Revisit your strategic career goal. Does it still make sense? Do you currently have two to three career options?
- Revisit your next right career step. Does it still make sense?
- Are the emotional, social and professional reasons still valid?
- Consider your progress to date. Are you still moving toward the destination?
- Revisit the N = Negotiate It questions. Do the assumptions, timetable and resources still stand?
- Consider your network and support group. Do members know where you're heading? Are they still on board and rowing in the same direction as you?

5. Play the role of the position you seek.

SNAPP™ shot

"Example is not the main thing in leading others; it's the only thing."

—Albert Schweitzer

To convince others—and yourself – that you're capable of handling the role to which you aspire, start practicing it today. There are two steps: (1) convince yourself you're up to the part; and (2) by your actions, convince others.

Success tip 10-7:

KEEP FIT

By some estimates, the majority of people trying to climb the corporate ladder are out of shape. If you take good care of yourself, you'll be ahead of the crowd. You will be able to start earlier, last longer and think more clearly. You'll be more optimistic and probably smile more often which will make you more engaging and cause more people to want to follow your lead.

Most physical fitness programs stress the following:

- Healthy diet
- Regular, appropriate exercise
- Avoidance of substances such as nicotine and excess alcohol
- Plenty of sleep.

How you keep fit is up to you, but it ought to be a daily priority.

Convince yourself

You began this in S = See It when you envisioned yourself in your strategic career and your next right career step. Ask yourself what you're doing, saying – even wearing. As you imagine yourself in the new role, what are others around you saying and doing? If you're having trouble "seeing" yourself in the part, try adopting a role model – a stellar performer with whom you're familiar. Consider what he/she is doing that you can emulate. Consider how you will need to change to reach that point. Then start acting the part.

Convince others

If you want to be accepted and "hired" for different roles involving increasing responsibilities, you must begin playing the part even before you get it. In so doing, you can become a role model for others. Being a role model does not depend on job title, organizational level, degree of education or even age. Anyone who takes on the attributes of an E^3 individual can be a role model and leader of others.

In general, role models and leaders are individuals who live a "can-do" rather than a "can't do" attitude. Here are a few examples:

"Can't do" (Follower)		"Can do" (Leader)
Play the victim	vs.	Survive and thrive
"It's good enough."	vs.	"How great can we make it?"
Take credit for success	vs.	Give credit for success
Expect thanks	vs.	Say "thanks"
Keep the news	vs.	Share the news
Frown	vs.	Smile
Complain	vs.	Take action
Resist change	vs.	Welcome change
Waste time	vs.	Manage time
Wait	vs.	Seek
Laissez faire	vs.	Prepare

Success tip 10-8:

OVER 40? FORGET ABOUT AGE!

There was a time when employees over 40 years of age – especially women – thought their career advancement opportunities were nearly over.

One of the best aspects of the new world of employment is that this is no longer the case. As long as the "Over 40s" follow a few simple guidelines when positioning themselves and their careers, there is no reason why E^3 employees cannot set their career sights as high as they like. The tips are:

- Dress tastefully and contemporarily. That includes hairstyle, lens frames and fashion accessories.
- If you're out of shape, initiate a fitness program. You'll have more energy and look better in your contemporary clothing.
- In discussions about your experience and skills, focus on your knowledge, expertise, accomplishments and energy – not on the length of your tenure at a particular company or the number of years you have held positions. Don't talk much about "how we used to do things."
- Develop war stories about your role in projects that brought about positive changes and results within your department and organization.
- As much as possible, keep up with both business and consumer technologies.
- Adopt a contemporary sport, hobby or interest.
- As one of your role models and/or mentors, adopt a younger fast-track E^3 employee and career manager.

P.S. These guidelines apply to everyone. As an E^3, you are likely to be ever marketable, almost without regard to age.

♣ **Ellee changes her image.**

Ellee notices that when employees of Global Products Division get together, their talk often turns to world markets, politics and the global economy. They all seem knowledgeable about geography, and many have traveled widely for both business and pleasure.

Ellee recognizes that if she is to fit in with these new colleagues, she will have to upgrade her water cooler conversation to include world events. She decides to let her subscription to U.S.-based news magazines subside and instead begin reading The Economist *and* The International Herald Tribune. *As she gains knowledge about world affairs, she builds confidence in her abilities to perform effectively in the Global Products Division once she is accepted.*

As manager of her current department, Ellee recognizes the importance of her leadership in keeping the team focused on quality, productivity and cooperation. She always tries to set an upbeat, positive tone, even on days when she's feeling stressed and over-worked. Her manner communicates that while she is fully committed to meeting department objectives, this job is not her last stop at T-TC. Therefore, she gives equal consideration to the greater corporation in everything she does, and she encourages other team members to do the same. Because Ellee has benefited from excellent mentoring in her career – from individuals both inside and outside T-TC – she makes herself available to mentor others. She also keeps her eye out for star potential in people who report to her. She intends to open the right doors for them in the future.

Summary

P = Persist is the most demanding and time-consuming of all the SNAPP™ steps because it involves:

- Minding the details and keeping score of the results, something most people dislike. It never ends.
- Ongoing recruiting and maintenance of a corps of qualified contacts in an ever-widening network.
- Communicating on a number of levels. It requires attention and skill, and despite its importance is often disliked and neglected.
- Staying focused on goals by devoting time each week, month and quarter to various aspects of career management. It is particularly difficult to plan ahead when you're in a job and career you particularly enjoy.
- Playing the role of the next position to which you aspire in order to convince yourself and others that you're up to the tasks.

Success tip 10-9:

KEEP YOUR BRIDGES INTACT

In today's fast-paced business environment, turnover is constant – within and among companies, industries and professions. The cliché about a "small world" is true. Try to avoid burning bridges. Your self-made "enemy" can show up anywhere, costing you the job, promotion, referral or opportunity.

Here are some things to keep in mind on a day-by-day and project-by-project basis:

- Never underestimate an adversary.
- Never send a nasty letter in anger or frustration. No matter how good it may feel at the time, never document feelings that belittle, criticize, degrade or blame. Never write a memo that is cynical, hurtful or unkind.
- Never say negative things about customers or other people in your organization, industry or profession. No matter how tempting, don't bond with complainers. If you are included in a gripe session, you can remain silent and discreetly change the subject, or make an excuse and leave. The next time you're invited to lunch with a complainer, have "other plans" or make an agreement ahead of time that you won't talk business.
- Use restraint with alcohol when socializing with customers and colleagues. When under the influence, you're more likely to reveal thoughts you'll later regret.
- Don't go drinking after work with your co-workers; it's a temptation to gossip. Instead, reserve free time for family and friends.
- Stay out of office politics; it's risky business. Instead, at all times perform as an enterprising employee. If you're in the right organization, stellar performance and leadership will win in the end.
- If you are passed over for a promotion or opportunity or if your job is terminated, proceed with grace and dignity. Analyze any mistakes you may have made, and learn from them. Resist the urge to blame others. Then try to look forward, not back.

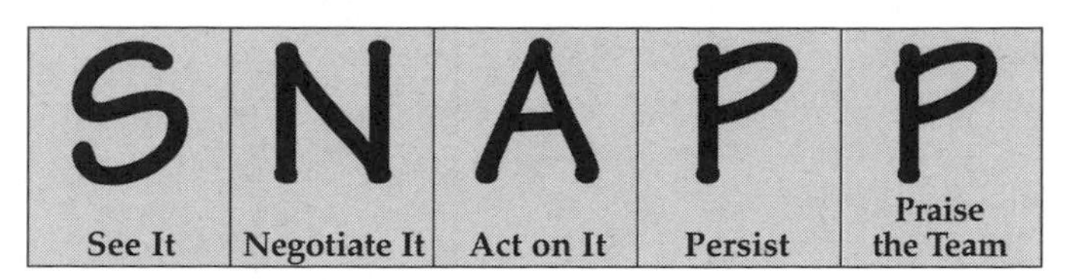

Chapter 11: P = Praise the Team

SNAPP™ shot

Your team members will fully support you only if they like you.

Although "praise the team" is presented as the final step in SNAPP™, it should never be left until last. Praise makes everyone feel good (including you), and the return on investment is unparalleled. When performed effectively, praise is the gift that keeps on giving in your current position and all those to come.

The P = Praise the Team steps are:

1. Make it a plus.
2. Say thank you.
3. Close and celebrate.

1. Make it a plus.

As noted earlier, you cannot reach your career goals alone. You need a team. To be a successful career manager, you must be both recruiting and working to retain members at all times. Often, the people on your team will be volunteers, helping you only because they like you, because the project is high-profile or inherently fun, because there's something in it for them – or all of the above.

Your success in enlisting the support of others will depend on all of your E^3 abilities:

- **Entrepreneurial:** In general, people like to associate with leaders who have a vision and know how to communicate it. It's natural to want to jump on the bandwagon.
- **Excellent:** If you want people's full support in your effort, you need to be credible so they'll continue the association, choose you for teams and be willing to make unqualified endorsements of your capabilities.

Success tip 11-1:

BE NICE TO EVERYONE

You learned it at your mother's knee. It is as important in business as it is in other aspects of life.

True leaders use the same treatment for everyone – from the security guard at the front entrance to the CEO on the top floor, from the person who delivers the sandwiches to the chair of the board of directors.

Wise and true leaders:

- Recognize the importance of everyone in the organization.
- Are more than polite; they treat everyone as worthy and special, including carrying through on promises every time and on time.
- Make an attempt to know and use everyone's name.
- Make allies of their peers' subordinates.

Leaders are the people that others want to follow, not the people they have to obey.

- **Engaging:** Unless you are likeable and easy to get along with, you will have a tough time recruiting and retaining your team. It's just that simple.

Once recruited, team members will participate only so long as the project is fun and they feel involved. Keep the team informed. Tell them the positives more often than the negatives. Serving on your team should be a privilege, not a pain.

➠ SNAPP™ it!

Make supporting your career project a pleasure. Try these tactics on a regular basis.

- Be subtle in reminding team members of what's in it for them when you succeed. For example, members of your network will benefit from important new contacts, family members may enjoy additional perks and everyone will get a pat on the back.
- Keep team members visible. Talk behind their backs, saying only complimentary things. It builds trust and morale and increases the odds people will remain on the team.
- By your words and deeds, let people know you respect and value their contributions.
- Accept advice with enthusiasm. You don't always have to follow it, but accept it gratefully. This is not deceitful; you can be sincerely grateful for the thoughtfulness and effort.

♣ Ellee positively positions her campaign.

Ellee knows that her boss Frank is in one of the best positions to help her progress in her career. She makes sure that Frank knows her intentions, and positions her move to Global Products Division as a benefit to the Domestic Products Division. She reminds Frank of the need for the two divisions to work together and how helpful it would be to have a Domestic Products Division ally working within Global.

She also enlists the support of colleagues in the Global Products Division. She is honest about her interest in their work and enthusiastic about the possibility of joining them. Her work almost speaks for itself. Ellee has served on several cross-functional, cross-division projects with Alf, a peer manager in Global Products Division. Recently they led a joint efficiency effort that resulted in an estimated savings of $2 million per year. Ellee tells Alf about her goal of transferring to Global Products Division, reminds him of their successful working relationship and expresses her hope that together they can continue to make solid contributions to T-TC.

Success tip 11-2:

SAY "THANKS" AT LEAST ONCE A DAY

Make it a habit to think of at least one person you will thank each day. Write the name on your to-do list. Don't let the day end without saying thanks to that person. Be sure you say thanks to different people, not always the same ones. If you cannot do it in person, use the phone or e-mail.

Can't think of someone to thank today? Look around you. Find someone who makes your life better. How about the lobby security guard who is particularly diligent about screening visitors? The counter person who remembers to serve your coffee just the way you like it? The receptionist who gets you into the office of the person you need to see? The colleague who shares a trade secret that works? (Be sure to tell him/her the results.) Someone in your family?

Surprise people and yourself with sincere thanks. You'll see how eager people are to be on your team and do their best for you.

2. Say thank you.

SNAPP™ shot

Those who give cheerfully give twice – once to others, once to themselves.

—Anonymous

To keep your supporters on your side, you must say thank you. And don't leave it to chance. It's too important.

On a daily basis, say thank you to everyone who helps you, regardless of their level or yours. Remember to thank your boss.

With regard to your career, thank your team for leads, referrals and every tip and piece of advice. Promptly send thank-yous for direct assistance such as interviews, information and introductions to key people.

Send thank-yous to organizations that allow you to speak, people who allow you to take them to lunch, co-workers who lend a hand and managers and mentors who take the time to assist and support. Send thank-yous for attempts at help, even when the deal doesn't pan out.

There's no *one best way* for saying thanks. Thanks can be as informal as a phone call or e-mail. They can be as formal as personally written notes. For important thank-yous, e-mail is acceptable as long as you follow with a written note. As an engaging person, you will be attuned to the most appropriate method in each case.

The most important things to remember about thank-yous are:

- Be prompt. Within 24 hours is optimal.
- Be specific. Tell people why you're thanking them and the expected or actual results.
- Be sincere. To offer insincere or undeserved praise is worse than saying nothing at all.

Success tip 11-3:

SUPPORT YOUR HOME TEAM

Some of the most important people on your team never go to your office. They are your network of family and friends. They deserve just as much tender loving care as your most valued customers and associates.

Make time for the people who sustain you, regardless of your current employer and the economic environment.

Avoid taking work home from the office as a regular routine. Show family and friends the same courtesy and respect you demonstrate to your most valued customers. Be polite and treat them as special. Give them the edge when it's a toss-up over time at the office versus time away. Always take vacations to refresh yourself personally and to remind your loved ones why they continue to support you.

Your home team is one of your most valuable life-long assets. Generally, it is the source of your greatest pleasure and pain. Without the support of the home team, almost no one can succeed.

➡ SNAPP™ it!

As you thank people for their help in furthering your career, be sure to make the thanks specific. Express your appreciation in person or on the phone, in an e-mail or formal note. If you like lists and forms, you can use one like this to plan and then track your thank-yous:

Thank you!	Team member	Specific contribution	Thank you date
☐			
☐			
☐			
☐			

♣ Ellee thanks her team.

As an engaging, excellent and entrepreneurial employee, Ellee makes it a habit to say at least one targeted "thanks" per day to the people with whom she regularly works. For example, even through she and Alf are peers and led a project together, Ellee sends Alf a hand-written note telling him specifically what she appreciated about his contributions to the project.

On days she has contact with members of her career support group, Ellee includes them in her to-do list of thank-yous. Saying "thanks" is often a mood-lifter for Ellee when she remembers the people on her team who are working to help her succeed.

3. Close and celebrate.

When you reach your important milestones and the next right step, it's cause for celebration. You didn't accomplish them alone; many people helped. A celebration brings closure and offers another opportunity to praise the team.

Celebrations can take many forms. They do not have to involve parties or excessive expense. Meaningful SNAPP™ celebrations can be as simple as hand-written notes. They can be as elaborate as dinners at the Ritz. As an entrepreneurial, excellent and engaging career manager, you'll be attuned to your own budget as well as the preferences of your individual team members.

Whatever you decide to do in celebration, a personal and specific "thanks" – written or spoken – is the minimal requirement.

➠ SNAPP™ it!

At minimum, take these steps within a week of starting a new position or job.

- Send thank-you notes to everyone who helped. There are no exceptions, even if the numbers are multiples of ten.
- If you cannot send hand-written notes to everyone, prioritize. Send them to the people who helped the most. Send e-mail or call the others.
- When sending word-processed letters, try to avoid the form letter look. Personalize each one with a short hand-written note.
- Stage a celebration with food and fun for family, friends and supporters, if appropriate.

Summary

P = Praise the Team requires energy and an ever upbeat attitude – not just at project end, but throughout the effort.

As an enterprising E^3 career manager, you will understand that the steps fall neatly into the three "E" areas:

- **Make it a plus.** Positioning the career project as a plus so your network of supporters is eager to assist you (entrepreneurial).
- **Say thank you.** Giving credit where it's due and allowing your supporters to shine (excellent).
- **Close and celebrate.** Saying sincere "thanks" and celebrating the victories (engaging).

Effectively praising the team will not only help you achieve your career goals, but also help win friends and allies that can last a lifetime.

♣ Epilogue

Thanks to her E^3 attributes and a well-crafted and executed strategy, Ellee's career stayed close to plan. She was successful in getting the transfer to Global Products Division as a product manager.

Two years later, just as she was beginning to feel a tinge of boredom with the job and think about moving on to the next career step, an opportunity to speak at a global marketing conference finally materialized. Because she had boosted her credibility by writing – and having published – several journal articles, Ellee was asked to deliver one of the high-profile presentations. The speech was a hit, attended by some major industry bigwigs who found her presentation innovative, insightful and witty.

The CEO of Wireless Wire Corporation, a major competitor of T-TC, initiated a conversation with Ellee following the speech. They discussed general topics about the industry, the global economy and the future of wireless communications. Always prepared with her positioning pitch, Ellee was also able to clearly articulate her career aspirations when asked. Shortly thereafter, Ellee was offered a tempting position in the Global Products Division at Wireless Wire. She accepted, even though it meant relocation to another city for her and the twins.

After a successful and fulfilling 13-year career at Wireless Wire during which she continued to grow professionally and contribute to substantial gains for the telecommunications giant, Ellee decided it was time to "go solo" and form her own marketing company. She resigned from Wireless Wire, and three months later "hung out her sign" as an independent marketing consultant.

Results are not yet in, but the outlook is excellent. With sterling E^3 attributes and skills, a vast network of supporters and SNAPP™, she almost cannot fail. Her first client, in fact, is likely to be the Tele-tele Corporation, with which she remains on excellent terms.

Chapter 12: It Isn't Easy. Start Now.

"It took me 20 years to become an overnight success."
—Eddie Cantor, entertainer (1892-1964)

Now you know what it looks like to be an enterprising employee and career manager. If you've been following along and working through the SNAPP™ It exercises, you know your strategic career goal and you have a workable action plan to get you there. You're off to a great start.

Just because you have a destination and a path, however, it doesn't mean it will necessarily be easy. Most people have to consciously and consistently work at success – in their careers and everything else that's worthwhile. Effective career management isn't something you do once or even once in a while. It requires small steps, practiced daily. The good news is that with practice, the steps become second nature.

If you remember nothing else from this book, please keep in mind these four key messages:

#1: You have to be good. It's the basis for everything else. Enterprising, E^3 employees and career managers are entrepreneurial, excellent and engaging. The more you embody all three attributes, the greater the likelihood of your career success.

#2: You have to prioritize. You cannot do everything you'd like to do. And you cannot do everything at once. There are a few big things that matter most. Figure out what they are and nail them. Without priorities and focus, you cannot accomplish your goals.

#3: You have to have a process. While SNAPP™ provides the framework, it isn't an exact recipe. You'll have to make up some things as you go along. Neither is SNAPP™ a guarantee that your career will end up exactly as you think it should in five, ten or twenty years. Interesting twists in the economy, your industry and YOU will change your decisions along the way. What's very sure, however, is that if you ignore these steps – whether or not you call them SNAPP™ – you'll miss being all you can be and such career highlights as the high esteem of your personal and professional team and the opportunity to make a difference in something that's truly important to you.

#4: Whatever you do, be passionate about it. Life is too short not to enjoy what you're doing.

Becoming an enterprising E^3 employee and career manager isn't easy, but the benefits are great. There's no time like the present. Start now.

SNAPP™ shot

Success begins in our minds. Then it becomes our process. Our habits determine our futures.

Appendix A: Index of Success Tips

Chapter 8: N = Negotiate It

Chapter 9: A = Act on It

Chapter 10: P = Persist

Chapter 11: P = Praise the Team

Appendix B: Suggested Reading

Biagi, Ron and Tresa Eyres. *Make It Happen! SNAPP™ Your Way to Success in Business and in Life*. It's the How, 2000.

Buford, Bob. *Half Time: Changing Your Game Plan from Success to Significance*. Zondervan, 1994.

Goleman, Daniel. *Emotional Intelligence*. Bantam Books, 1997.

Goleman, Daniel. *Working with Emotional Intelligence*. Bantam Doubleday Dell Publications, 2000.

Hanratty, Donald J., Ron Biagi and Tresa Eyres. *Career Continuation: Make it a SNAPP™*. It's the How, 2001.

Hansen, Richard. *Credibility Power: The Art of Selling Yourself*. Prestonwood Press, 2001.

Peters, Tom. *The Brand You 50: Or, Fifty Ways to Transform Yourself from 'Employee' into a Brand That Shouts Distinction, Commitment and Passion!* Knopf, 1999.

Senge, Peter M. *The Fifth Discipline: The Art & Practice of The Learning Organization*. Doubleday/Currency, 1990.

Stoltz, Paul G. *Adversity Quotient: Turning Obstacles into Opportunities*. John Wiley & Sons, Inc. 1997.

Stoltz, Paul G. *Adversity Quotient @ Work*. William Morrow, 2000.

Walker, Jean Erickson. *The Age Advantage: Making the Most of Your Midlife Career Transition*. Berkley Books, 2000.

Weiss, Alan. *Million Dollar Consulting: The Professional's Guide to Growing a Practice*. McGraw Hill, 1997.

S	N	A	P	P™

Career Management is a SNAPP™

Planning Stage

S = See It

1. What does it look like when I've got it right?
2. Why do I want this?
3. Who else cares and why?
4. What do I have to offer?
5. What knowledge, skills and abilities will I need?

N = Negotiate It

1. What is the scope of the effort?
2. What are the assumptions?
3. Who will help?
4. What can change or go wrong?
5. What are the financial implications?

A = Act on It

1. What's the action plan?
2. Who is accountable?
3. Who will support it?

Implementation Stage

P = Persist

1. Mind the details and keep score.
2. Recruit and retain your team.
3. Develop and maintain a communications package.
4. Stay focused.
5. Play the role of the position you seek.

P = Praise the Team

1. Make it a plus.
2. Say thank you.
3. Close and celebrate.